Cranbr

rk. S.M.

Clark.

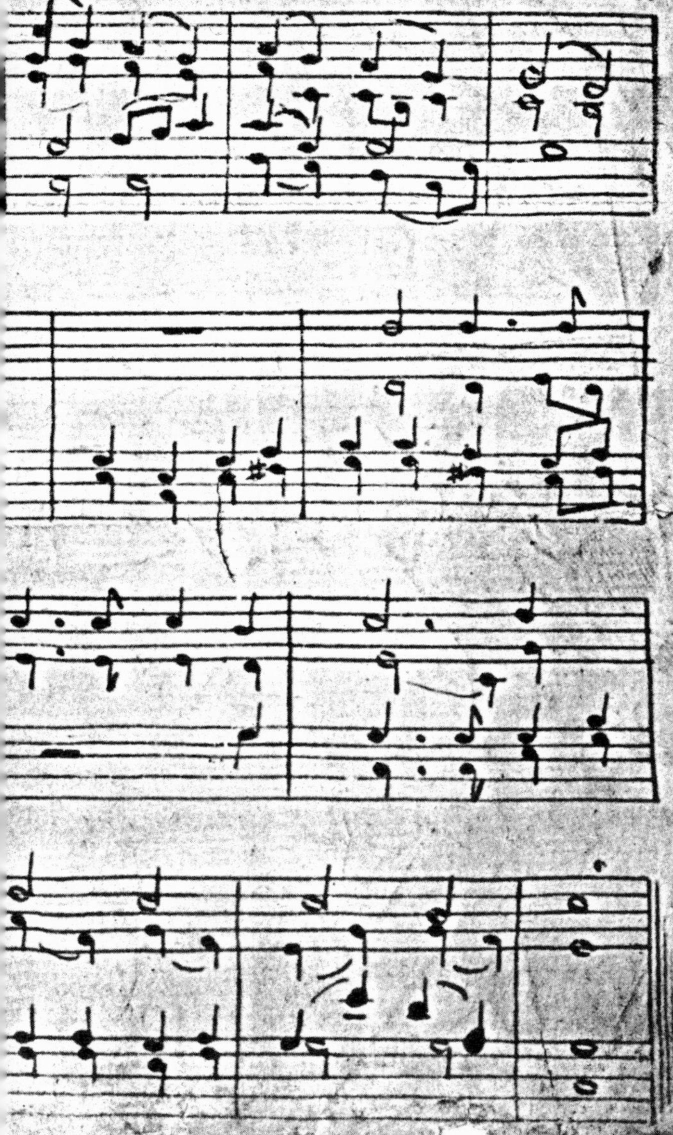

BASIC BROAD YORKSHIRE

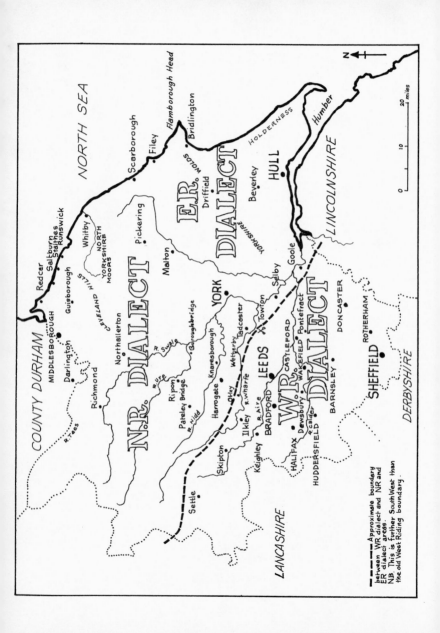

BASIC BROAD YORKSHIRE

Arnold Kellett

Smith
Settle

First published in 1991 by
Smith Settle Ltd
Ilkley Road
Otley
West Yorkshire
LS21 3JP

Reprinted 1992

Revised edition 1992

ISBN 1 870071 82 4

Frontispiece:
Map of Yorkshire showing the dialect boundaries

Designed, printed and bound by
SMITH SETTLE
Ilkley Road, Otley, West Yorkshire LS21 3JP

Contents

Dedication

Dedicated to all who love the ancient speech of Yorkshire, this book is also in memory of my father, who contributed to it substantially and enjoyed reading it before publication.

Acknowledgements

Thanks are due to the following for permission to quote prose or verse, or use illustrations: the Yorkshire Dialect Society (*Transactions* and *Summer Bulletin*), *Dalesman*, *Telegraph and Argus*, *Evening Courier*, Leeds University, Leeds Central Library, Bill Cowley, Ruth Dent, Norman Duerden, Sydney Martin and Geoffrey Robinson.

I am also indebted to various good Yorkshire folk for constructive comments and elucidations: Irwin Bielby, Jack Danby OBE, Ruth and John Dent, Jean and Stanley Evans, Alan Hardill, Audrey and Peter Houlston, N A Hudleston, Arthur Kinder, Jim Savage, Cedric Sellers, Muriel Shackleton, Gwen Wade.

I am particularly grateful to Stanley Ellis, the well-known dialect expert, for giving this book his imprimatur and kindly providing a foreword.

Thanks are also due to Peter Kearney for the maps and 'coat of arms'.

Once again, many thanks to my wife, Pat, who has been moithered by the word-processor at a time she should have been enjoying the arrival of her eleventh grandchild.

Author's Note

This revised edition includes many additional words in the extended Yorkshire Dictionary section. A considerable number of these have been kindly suggested by readers, and the author would be pleased to hear of further words or phrases via the publishers.

Foreword

'Yorkshire Dialect' is so special that it seems to have become the property of the whole country more than the local talk of any county. Most people feel they know it when they hear it. They don't all love it, they certainly don't all understand it, but they accept that it exists.

The belief that Yorkshire dialect is a single entity poses problems when you try to define what it is. It's not one, but many; books small enough and readable enough to give the real information about the varieties and nuances of Yorkshire dialect are few and far between. Perhaps the best ones in the past have been the simple word-lists that have given a great deal of pleasure to both Yorkshire folk and others. Academic books that are special and need training to sort out, have been written by scholars, but few want to wade through all that.

Dr Arnold Kellett is trying another way. Using his skill as a teacher of foreign languages he has realised that readers can come to terms with the parts of the language simply set out, so that we can see the varying shapes of the words, depending on how and where they are used. In his task he has sought the help of dialect speakers from different parts of the county, and also consulted scholarly works. His own researches into local history have also been exploited.

He has kept his book reasonably short, but in this attempt to portray the broad sweep of difference and change, those who want to know more of Yorkshire dialect will find something to entertain, to intrigue, and perhaps to amaze.

Arnold Kellett and I were Scouts in competing troops in Bradford many years ago. Even as near as where he came from, they spoke different from where I came from. We used to say of his area that 't'ducks flew back'ards up theear to keep t'dust aht o ther een.' They say that and other things of outlandish places in various spots all over the world. Dr Kellett has identified quite a few of the Yorkshire ones in a very readable way.

Stanley Ellis
Hon Secretary, Yorkshire Dialect Society

A New Approach to Broad Yorkshire

The term 'broad Yorkshire' was originally coined to describe the great size of the county, by far the biggest in England, with the claim that there are more acres in Yorkshire than there are letters in the Bible. If you care to check this you will find that the King James's Bible contains 3,566,840 letters – easily outmatched by Yorkshire's 3,923,359 acres. No wonder that Christopher Saxton, when he published the first real map of Yorkshire in 1577, proclaimed in Latin on the title-page 'The County of York . . . in length, breadth and population more distinguished than all the rest'.

As Saxton was a Yorkshireman, born near Morley, it is understandable that he drew attention to the fact that his own county required a larger map than any of the others he produced. But it is not a matter of mere 'broad acres'. Yorkshire has always been impressive because it is large enough to encompass such a variety of scenery – from the Pennine hills and dales of the west to the cliffs and beaches of the eastern coastal face; from the largely industrial south to the agricultural north, with further contrasts, such as that between the rugged, heather-clad moors and the rolling Plain of York.

This extensive and varied terrain partly explains why Yorkshire speech differs from one part of the county to another – indeed, sometimes from one valley to another, and even from one town or village to another. Yet the various branches of the Yorkshire dialect family have sufficient in common to have been regarded as a single, distinctive language, with the result that the term 'broad Yorkshire' now refers, not to the county itself, but to the dialect of its inhabitants.

A book about this dialect has, I believe, a two-fold topicality. First, the concept of 'broad Yorkshire' as a language helps to preserve the notion that the old, familiar county – Saxton's 'County of York' – continues to exist in spite of all the bureaucratic changes. Yorkshire owes its origin mainly to the Vikings, who in the ninth century, from the settlement of Jorvik (York), divided their vast territory into three parts, each called a 'thridding' or third, later known as the ridings. These lasted for more than a thousand years – and then, on April Fools Day 1974, the County of York ceased to exist as an administrative entity, and was amputated, dismembered and subdivided, the three ancient ridings being officially abolished.

Yet, in spite of what appears on modern maps and envelopes, underneath this superficial labelling there is still the original Yorkshire, with the unifying common language of its dialect. It is not because of any attempt to turn back the bureaucratic clock, but because of the need for accurate terminology, that the Yorkshire Dialect Society continues to describe the three main branches of Yorkshire dialect by the standard terms North Riding, East Riding and West Riding. So, first, a renewed interest in 'broad Yorkshire' is very much part of the current movement to preserve Yorkshire identity.

The second reason why this book seems topical, and even a matter of urgency, is that the dialect of Yorkshire, like all dialects, is under threat of extinction. Just as our green spaces and fine old buildings are constantly menaced by developers, so our time-honoured dialects are under continual pressure from the combined forces of education, the mass media, residential mobility and the importance of standard English in personal advancement – with many people having radically altered their native speech for social or career reasons.

There is nothing new about this. 'Modern education is making havoc with provincial dialects', wrote William Cudworth in the preface to his *Yorkshire Speyks*. This was as long ago as 1906. He would have been surprised and gratified to see how the dialect of Yorkshire, at least, has proved sufficiently robust to survive the rest of the century – though as a minority language, mostly in an attenuated form, and now largely replaced by what Stanley Ellis calls 'regional speech'.

Yet real Yorkshire dialect is still understood and cherished.

In preparing and checking *Basic Broad Yorkshire* I have been encouraged again and again by the number of people whose eyes light up at the sound of a distinctive Yorkshire word or phrase. They may not use dialect in everyday speech, but it is something they recall with delight as having been used by their parents or grandparents. Yorkshire dialect is an essential part of our heritage and culture, something unique that we must not allow to die by default. Dialect-speakers are an endangered species, with real scarcity value. At this critical period while they are still around, and while dialect is still remembered with an affectionate warmth, it seems to me vital that 'broad Yorkshire' should be captured and encapsulated in a book.

The novelty of the approach in *Basic Broad Yorkshire* is that it sets out to present Yorkshire dialect as a language in its own right, taking it absolutely seriously. This is quite simply a language text-book, a course in Yorkshire dialect – a refresher course for native speakers, and an introductory course for those outside the county, and those within it who have lost touch with the speech of their ancestors.

Above all *Basic Broad Yorkshire* is not a joke. I appreciate that there will always be people who find dialect irresistibly comical, and who may well regard Yorkshire dialect in particular as a quaint and clownish speech afflicting the loud-mouthed, slow-witted inhabitants of this enormous county in the barbaric North. 'Ah, yes! Broad Yorkshire,' they will say, 'Ee bah goom, and all that' – as they ignorantly cling to the stereotyped images of old chaps in cloth caps and mufflers, or backward yokels mucking out the cows.

This book – though by no means lacking in humour – is as far removed as possible from this superior let's-have-a-snigger-at-dialect approach, regrettably seen in booklets which exploit dialect as something only good for a giggle. On the contrary, the following chapters lay before the reader the basic components of a vigorous and venerable language, adding samples of verse and prose, both comic and serious, ranging from traditional and early classic pieces to work by contemporary

dialect writers. The concluding section is a Yorkshire Dictionary compiled not only to give the meaning of words and
phrases occurring in the book, but to serve as a practical guide
to Yorkshire dialect words in general.

My approach to 'broad Yorkshire' is, in fact, that of a former
teacher of modern languages, and this book is on similar lines
to school text-books, such as my *Basic French*, because it sets
out as simply and clearly as possible all the strange sounds,
curious words and enigmatic phrases of this 'foreign language'
in our midst. Lest anybody should regard this very approach
as a kind of gimmick, let me make a few preliminary points to
clear away some of the confusion and misunderstanding which
surrounds Yorkshire dialect:

1. *Yorkshire dialect is a virtually a foreign language in its spoken form*,
as far as speakers of standard English are concerned. It is not
just a question of accent and intonation. Actual dialect
contains the kind of vocabulary and idiom which makes it
largely incomprehensible to people outside the county – and
to an increasing number who pride themselves on being
Yorkshire born and bred. A fluent speaker of dialect, such as
a countryman from the North or East, or some old character
from the West Riding, can sound quite incomprehensible when
in full flood. Most such speakers will, however, modify their
speech for the benefit of unenlightened incomers, or **off-
comed-uns**, so that their general drift will be understood. Yet
the subtleties of meaning are missed, and colourful expression
unappreciated, by those who know no dialect.

So little can mean so much. For example, '**Nay, *lad***!' might
well be the equivalent of: 'I'm very disappointed in you, son.
I thought you would have been able to do better than this'.
Only patient study of dialect can break down this language
barrier in our midst.

2. *Yorkshire dialect is a virtually a foreign language in its written form.*
As dialect speakers become rarer, the written dialect of earlier

generations becomes less accessible. Give the average speaker of standard English a passage in the broad Yorkshire of a few generations ago, and it would be almost unintelligible. When readers come across snippets of Yorkshire speech in such works as Emily Brontë's *Wuthering Heights* or J B Priestley's *The Good Companions* there is obviously a need for correct understanding.

The challenge is all the greater when a whole story or poem is written entirely in Yorkshire dialect, and the meaning likely to be completely lost on the uninitiated. Just as some linguistic effort is needed to fully appreciate the dialect poems of Robert Burns, so a similar effort is required to enjoy poems in Yorkshire dialect – a number of them, incidentally, worthy to be compared with Burns.

Yorkshire dialect has not yet become a dead language, but even if it does, there will be every reason to study and comprehend it, just as we do Anglo-Saxon, Latin, Greek or Sanskrit, because of the cultural and literary gems that would otherwise be inaccessible to us.

3. *Yorkshire dialect needs to be appreciated as an ancient and honourable form of speech.* The dialect of Yorkshire has its roots in the languages of the early colonisers of the North – the Angles, the Vikings and the Norsemen. Only ignorance preserves the notion that 'broad Yorkshire' is a debased form of standard English. When a Yorkshireman says **ax** instead of 'ask', he is not making a stupid transposition of the consonants, but preserving the original form of the Anglo-Saxon verb **acsian**. When he says, for example, **Ah'm starved ter deeath** he is using the verb 'starve' in its original sense of to 'suffer intensely', in this case from the cold. He is, in fact, using part of the Anglo-Saxon verb *steorfan* (to die), still used in German as *sterben*, with its past tense *starb* so close to 'starve'. Also as in German he uses **oft** rather than 'often' – not a shortened form, but the original Anglo-Saxon word. Far from using the language incorrectly, a speaker of Yorkshire dialect often unconsciously preserves words and pronunciations used by his

ancestors, which have disappeared from modern English.

4. *Yorkshire dialect needs to be defined and classified.* On the one hand, dialect needs to be distinguished from rough, slovenly and ungrammatical speech, which retains a regional accent, with dropped 'h's' and 'g's', for example, but lacks all the colour and character of Yorkshire dialect, which has its own style, vocabulary and turns of phrase.

On the other hand, 'broad Yorkshire' itself needs to be appreciated in all its variety. Outside the county, people tend to assume that there is only one Yorkshire dialect, and that all Yorkshire people speak in more or less the same way. As we have seen, there are three main branches, named after the old ridings. These are really in two principal divisions. First, there is the speech of the West Riding, so vivid and forthright, and to some ears loud and strident, associated with the mills and mines of the industrial revolution. Secondly, there is the speech of the North and East Ridings, which is quieter and gentler, more associated with shepherds, farmers and village folk. In the Yorkshire Dialect Society both divisions of dialect are used, with no problem of communication – only the convention of appending to written dialect the abbreviation WR, NR or ER to indicate the riding.

There are considerable differences, mainly in vowel sounds, between WR dialect and what I have for convenience described in this book as NER (North and East Ridings) because of the close similarity between the speech of these two areas. Indeed, it is not always easy to distinguish between NR and ER. As Bill Cowley has pointed out in the introduction to his *Cleveland Anthology*, the dialect of Cleveland in the North Riding is scarcely different from that of much of the East Riding, and there is a greater difference between the east and west parts of the North Riding. In addition to the WR/NER divide there are pockets of local speech peculiar to such places as York, Hull or Barnsley, which still preserve the feeling of individuality in these communities.

5. *Yorkshire dialect deserves a better image.* 'Broad Yorkshire' has been the subject of prejudice, no doubt ever since it was first isolated by that name, and children at home and school were rebuked for using words like **summat** on the grounds that it was 'common'. It is to be hoped that now dialect has been reduced to a minority language its true value will be appreciated by the general public – and not merely by the members of the Yorkshire Dialect Society, the East Yorkshire Dialect Society and a number of individual enthusiasts. We need to fight tooth and nail the all-too-prevalent snobbery which sees 'broad Yorkshire' as quaint and comical, something which has a certain curiosity value, and an occasional use as entertainment, but nothing more. This is no way to treat the language of our forebears.

6. *Yorkshire dialect is in urgent need of a conservation policy.* Language is constantly evolving, and neither dialect nor regional speech can expect to remain immune from the influence of the media. To take just one example. Whatever happened to the word 'first'? This good Anglo-Saxon word of one syllable has recently been ousted by that silly word of four syllables 'initially'. At first (I refuse to write 'initially'!) it no doubt sounded rather high-class, like other importations, and became fashionable for that reason. Yet is it really preferable to the older and simpler word? This kind of affectation is threatening dialect, as well as good English in general. Words and phrases come in and take over, and those of us who want to keep dialect alive must be vigilant and zealous for its purity.

As well as the unconscious erosion caused by the media there is the deliberate suppression of dialect through education, especially when it is linked with the necessity to 'get on' by speaking the Queen's English. Yet there are fortunately many teachers who operate a bilingual policy, encouraging dialect and local speech outside the classroom, but insisting on standard English within it, and for formal occasions. There is no reason why we should not keep 'broad Yorkshire' as a living language, happily existing alongside standard English, and become like Southey's doctor who 'spoke the King's English in one circle and the King's Yorkshire in another'.

There are those who believe that dialect is doomed, and that however much it is safeguarded and promoted it will die with the generation that still speaks it. The fact is, though, that it is not only old folks who enjoy dialect. A survey I once conducted in a large North Yorkshire comprehensive school revealed a substantial number of children who regularly used dialect words such as **brass, gob, lugs, spice, bairn, laik, cow-clap, britches** (instead of 'trousers') **bray** (instead of 'hit') etc and many colloquial expressions that would not be understood outside Yorkshire.

As an optimistic conservationist I do not accept that dialect is on its death bed. The survival of Welsh and the revival of Manx show what can be done. There never has been an age like this, with such a widespread awareness of the need to conserve our heritage, including – let us hope – the heritage of Yorkshire dialect.

It should be added, as a final introductory point, that although my approach to 'broad Yorkshire' is from the analytical viewpoint of a teacher of languages, I can claim to be a 'native speaker'. I was born in the heart of the West Riding in the hill-top village of Wibsey, just south of Bradford, and only a mile or two from the territory of those two Halifax champions of dialect, John Hartley and, more recently, Wilfred Pickles. I grew up immersed in the wonderfully rich dialect of Wibsey folk, and have kept in touch with it ever since. In this I have been encouraged by my father, who in his nineties fondly recalled a boyhood when dialect was the everyday speech of working people in Wibsey. For example, when he went for his regular short-back-and-sides, it was quite normal for the barber to say to him: **'Nah 'od thi 'eead still, lad – else Ah s'll cut thi throit'.** Or he would quote his mother's observation on the rarety of filial gratitude: **'It's nut oft t' kitten brings t' cat a mahse.'**

But this book is not a sentimental journey back to my boyhood, or my father's. It is a factual presentation of Yorkshire dialect, which, if worked through systematically, rather than dipped into, should at least give you the full flavour of 'broad Yorkshire'.

The Origins and History of Yorkshire Dialect

The first British language of which we have any knowledge is that of the Celts, an early branch of the Indo-Europeans, who began to settle here around 500 BC. This language of the Ancient Britons survives in certain Yorkshire place-names and topographical features, for example, in the names of rivers such as the Calder, Crimple and Nidd, and in heights such as Penyghent and Otley Chevin. Very few Celtic words have survived in English. In Yorkshire dialect we have an occasional word like **brock** (badger), and a remnant of Celtic can be seen in the structure of numerals once traditionally used for counting sheep.

As a living language Celtic survives as Erse, Gaelic and especially Welsh, for the Celtic-speaking Britons were eventually pushed back into what is now Wales by the invading Angles and Saxons, whose word for 'foreigner', incidentally, gave us the term 'Welsh'.

It is in the language of the Angles – the original English – that Yorkshire dialect has its earliest roots. Once the Roman armies had finally withdrawn from Britain in AD 410, the country was left wide open for invasion and settlement by waves of people from northern Germany. These were mainly Angles and Saxons, but there were also Jutes and Frisians, who settled in Kent and other parts of the south.

The Angles came, according to St Bede, from Angulus – literally an angle or corner of land – in what we now know as Schleswig-Holstein. They eventually occupied the whole of Northumbria, the area north of the Humber, extending from that river up to the Firth of Forth. They also spread southwards through East Anglia and the Midlands as far as the Thames, this southern part of their territory becoming known as Mercia.

There was a difference between the speech of the Northumbrian and Mercian Angles (sometimes described as the

Northern and North Midlands dialects). Yorkshire originally spoke the Northumbrian dialect, but the dialect of Mercia later spread into the southern part of the county, giving the basis of the two main divisions of Yorkshire dialect: taking the River Wharfe as the approximate boundary between Mercian and Northumbrian speech, we have to the south the dialect of the West Riding (WR) and to the north the dialects of the North and East Ridings (NR and ER). These last two are closely related to each other and also have considerable affinity with other dialects of the old Northumbria, such as 'Geordie'.

Though there were differences between Mercian and Northumbrian, the more fundamental difference between the speech of the North and South of England results from the fact the Angles colonised mainly the north and east, whereas the Saxons – with a somewhat different speech – colonised the south and west. We tend to lump them together as the Anglo-Saxons, but it must not be forgotten that they were separate peoples, a situation which helped to lay the foundations of the 'north-south divide' still with us. Whilst Yorkshire was occupied by the Angles, the Saxons were the southerners and westerners, as can be seen from the areas named after them: Middlesex (Middle Saxons), Essex (East Saxons) Sussex (South Saxons) and Wessex (West Saxons).

Though Angles and Saxons spoke different dialects they could certainly understand each other, and Anglo-Saxon, or Old English, with its regional variations, became the standard literary language of England, lasting until 1066 and beyond. Compared with standard English, Yorkshire dialect preserves a high proportion of the Anglo-Saxon, with its broad vowels, short words and general atmosphere of strong Germanic speech. Typical of Anglo-Saxon words used in Yorkshire dialect, but no longer found in standard English, are, for example, the verb **sam** (to gather, pick up) from the Anglo-Saxon *samnian*, similar to modern German *sammeln*. Then there are words used in standard English, but which have kept their original Anglo-Saxon pronunciation only in dialect –

words such as **hoose** (house), **lang** (long) and **blinnd** (blind),

As has already been pointed out, dialect forms which at first sight seem to be corruptions or mispronunciations of English (**ax, starved** etc) are simply forms going back to Anglo-Saxon. The same is true of words like **nobbut** (only), which preserves the older 'nought but', from the Anglo-Saxon **nan-beutan**. Certain Anglo-Saxon plurals are still used in Yorkshire dialect, common examples of which are **childer** (children) and **een** (eyes). Terms which would instantly be recognised by our Anglian forefathers are, for example, the dialect words for cowshed – **mistal, byre** and **shippon**. Indeed, they would feel at home with the general pronunciation and intonation of 'broad Yorkshire', and the way it still uses the familiar form of 'you', **tha, thi, thine,** and **yon** or **yond** for 'that' and 'those'.

The difference between northern and southern English, and to a lesser extent the difference between NER and WR dialect, was intensified by a further series of invasions and colonisations starting in the ninth century. These invaders were from Scandinavia: first, the Danes, better known as the Vikings, and later the Norwegians, better known as the Norsemen. Their influence is seen in place-names (eg Muker, Gunnerside, and in village names ending in 'by', 'thorpe' or 'thwaite'), in the division of the county into three ridings, each subdivided into wapentakes, in various topographical terms (eg 'beck', 'fell', 'gill', 'carr') and in many items of Yorkshire vocabulary. To take just a few examples – **addle** (to earn), **kist** (wooden chest), **lig** (to lie), **laik** (to play), **laithe** (barn), **lug** (ear), **neave** (fist), **stee** (ladder) and **teem** (to pour). These are typical of words from Old Scandinavian, which increased the difference between Mercian and Northumbrian speech, adding Viking place-names of about 13% to the WR area, but to NR 28% and ER 40%.

When the French-speaking Normans (originally Norsemen themselves) began their occupation of England in 1066, the foundation was laid for the eventual absorption of Norman French into Anglo-Saxon, producing Middle English, the

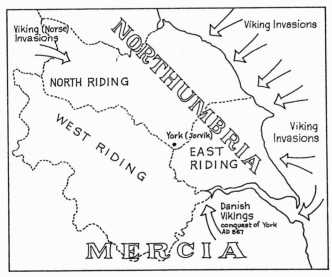

The Viking invasions of Yorkshire and its division into ridings.

language associated with Geoffrey Chaucer, for example, in the late fourteenth century. Yorkshire dialect shows very little Norman influence, no doubt because it originates in the language of working people, who had little contact with their French-speaking superiors. However, a few Norman French words no longer found in standard English have been preserved in Yorkshire dialect. For example: **arran** (spider) from *araignée*, **urchin** (hedgehog) from *hérisson*, **buffit** (small stool) from *buffet*, **fent** (a remnant of cloth) from *fendre* (to split) and **frume(n)ty** (dish made from wheat) from *froment* (wheat).

Until the late fifteenth century there was no standardised form of English, and people spoke and wrote in the dialect of their particular region. Examples of this in Yorkshire can be seen in medieval mystery plays from York and Wakefield, which, although they are literary productions in verse, include early examples of Yorkshire dialect. From 1476 (Caxton's press) printing began to establish a standard form of English, and the growing importance of London meant that the kind of English used by educated Londoners spread throughout the country.

As the centuries progressed, dialects continued to thrive alongside 'official' English, coming under its influence, and at the same time evolving on independent lines. But dialect was increasingly regarded as an inferior form of speech, all very well for country folk, labourers and servants, and later those who worked in the mines and mills, but something to be discarded and disparaged by the comparative few who were privileged to have a proper education. The great enemy of dialect was literacy, because as soon as a child was taught to read there was immediate contact with standardised English. From the reports of school inspectors as early as the 1850s we can see that there was a policy of discouraging dialect and strong local accent. Except for a few isolated cases, nothing was printed in Yorkshire dialect until the nineteenth century, and 'broad Yorkshire' survived alongside educated English as a dynamic oral tradition.

The few early printed examples of Yorkshire dialect, apart from word-lists such as John Ray's *Collection of Northern Words* (1674), were mostly in verse. There was, for example, *A Yorkshire Dialogue* (1683) by George Meriton, a Northallerton lawyer, and the Cleveland *Lyke-wake Dirge*, printed by John Aubrey in 1686, but very much older. Several dialect poems and songs appeared in the eighteenth century, and especially in the early nineteenth century, inspired by the example of Robert Burns (see pp109-113). But Yorkshire dialect prose did not appear in print to any extent until the emergence of the broadsheets, annuals and almanacks produced for the workers of the West Riding.

The first of these was Abel Bywater's *Wheelswarf Chronicle* (1830), followed by his *Shevvild Chap's Annual* (1836). Then came *The Bairnsla Foakes' Annual an' Pogmoor Olmenack*, produced by

'Tom Treddlehoyle', alias Charles Rogers of Barnsley, first appearing in 1843 and running till the end of the century. A substantial amount of dialect had been used by Emily Brontë in *Wuthering Heights* (1847), but the average dialect-speaker was far more likely to read the cheap, light-hearted paperback annuals which gained tremendous popularity in the second half of the century. In 1852 appeared *T'Frogland Olmenac an' Leeds Loiners' Annual*, and in 1867 the most famous of them all, *The Clock Almanac*, almost every issue entirely written by John Hartley of Halifax for a period of fifty years.

Between 1870 and 1881 no fewer than eighteen different dialect almanacks were published in the West Riding, and later there were others outside the area, such as *T' Nidderdill Olminac* of 1886. These almanacks had an immense circulation and influence, because the almanack content (calendar, dates of notable events, phases of the moon etc) was of less interest than the dialect content in both prose and verse. Much of the humour has dated, but these almanacks are fascinating as social documents and show Yorkshire dialect in its prime, enjoying the boost of availability in print at prices affordable by the working classes. (*The Clock Almanac*, for example, with its coloured covers, and the Leeds *Tommy Toddless Comic Almenac*, each cost only threepence.)

In the early part of the twentieth century, though *The Clock Almanac* continued to appear, dialect was more likely to be read in occasional poems or stories in newspapers, some of which published weekly dialect features such as the humorous tales by 'Buxom Betty' in the *Bradford Telegraph and Argus*, and more recently topical verse by 'Owd Joss' (Geoffrey Robinson) in the *Hull Daily Mail*. Until the 1940s, dialect recitations such as *Ahr Mary's Bonnet* could frequently be heard on the amateur stage, in Sunday School concerts, for example. Dialect comedies by such writers as J R Gregson, F A Carter, George Taylor and Wylbert Kemp were also popular on the amateur stage, and occasionally dialect plays were broadcast. Certain Yorkshire novelists made use of dialect, notably J S Fletcher,

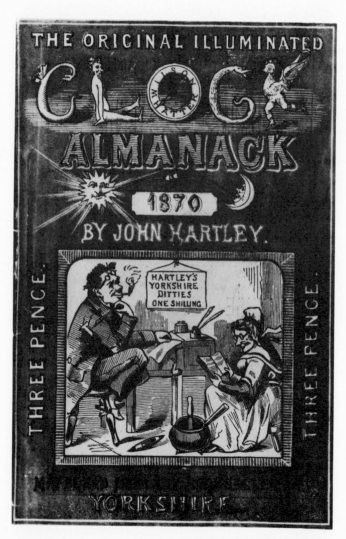

Two Victorian dialect almanacks.

Price Thrippence.

Halliwell Sutcliffe, Edward Booth, William Riley, Phyllis Bentley and J B Priestley, the latter's Jess Oakroyd in *The Good Companions* speaking the dialect of Bruddersford (Bradford). A good example of a contemporary novelist who makes use of Yorkshire dialect is Stan Barstow of Ossett.

Professional comedians such as Tom Foy, 'Stainless Stephen' and Albert Modley often used Yorkshire dialect in their performances, and in recent years colourful WR speech has been the medium of the comedian Charlie Williams. Wilfred Pickles OBE of Halifax (1907-1978), on both radio and television, did much to popularise Yorkshire speech throughout the nation, his canny yet genial personality giving the county considerable publicity.

In recent years interest in dialect has been encouraged by local radio and publications such as the *Dalesman* (founded in 1939), with the realistic little 'Young Fred' poems by Will Clemence and the remarks of 'Amos'. Creative dialect writing has been especially encouraged by the Yorkshire Dialect Society – though the latter came into existence as an off-shoot of serious academic research rather than from any idea of encouraging poets and authors. A few years before the formation of the YDS in 1897, dialect studies had been immeasurably enriched by the pioneer work of Joseph Wright of Windhill, Shipley. He was a real dialect-speaker who had started work at the age of six as a donkey-boy in the quarries, yet such was his determination and brilliance that he ended up as Professor of Comparative Philology at Oxford. In 1891 Joseph Wright took over the million slips of vocabulary assembled by Professor W W Skeat, and by 1905 he had published at his own expense his monumental six volume *English Dialect Dictionary*. The committee which had helped Joseph Wright to collect Yorkshire dialect material formed the nucleus of the YDS.

Still very much a going concern, the society is keeping authentic Yorkshire dialect alive by regular meetings, such as the Christmas Crack, where members read poems and tales,

Joseph Wright.

often their own compositions. It also promotes dialect by means of publications and its journals, *Transactions* and *Summer Bulletin*. *Transactions* publishes both creative material and academic articles on Yorkshire dialect, and amongst its editors have been distinguished dialect experts such as F W Moorman, W J Halliday and Professor Harold Orton, the last two being joint editors of the first volume of the *Survey of English Dialects* (1962). Harold Orton was Professor of English Language at Leeds University (1946-64), providing a close link between the university and the YDS, which still continues.

This brief survey of the history of Yorkshire dialect would not be complete without some comment on the state of dialect today. An idea of the dialect literature available is given in the bibliography, a small selection from a variety of material from all over the county, ranging from YDS reprints of earlier publications to work by contemporary writers. What interests us, though, is how much dialect is still being used as a form of communication. To what extent is 'broad Yorkshire' still spoken?

The answer given is inevitably based on personal experience and impression. There has been no systematic survey of the whole of Yorkshire to attempt to measure the extent to which dialect is spoken, or at least understood. In his *Dialect and Accent in Industrial West Yorkshire* (1985) K M Petyt, surveying mainly Bradford, Halifax and Huddersfield, came to the conclusion that most speakers were to be identified by their accent rather than actual dialect, though he found a small amount of dialect still in common use – words like **summat, nowt, lass, lad, aye, nay, laik,** and constructions such as **an' all** and **give over**. A minority of older people have a much wider vocabulary than this, and will use dialect occasionally, such as when making a humorous point or chatting about old times with their friends, but as everyday speech there can be no doubt that full-blown dialect is no longer used by the vast majority in urban West Yorkshire.

When we think of the huge population of the old West

Riding, with its large cities and conurbations, it is worth pointing out that though dialect is retained only by a small minority here, this minority may amount to a significant number. On the other hand, the old North and East Ridings have smaller populations, but their largely rural character might suggest that there is likely to be a much higher proportion of dialect-speakers. A survey conducted in 1986, based on the College of Ripon and York St John, of villages between York and Selby showed that the most characteristic of the ER vowel sounds were no longer being used, though the researchers found a regionally distinctive form of speech, with a knowledge of words such as **fettle**, **flit**, **hame**, **pluf**, **shoon**, **teem**, **theeak** and **yat**. In preparing this book I have come to the conclusion that many people in rural areas – including children – still have a knowledge of dialect, though they may be shy about using it in the presence of people from outside their region.

We have noted in the previous chapter William Cudworth's concern about the survival of dialect as far back as 1906. Half-way through the century, in 1954, that close observer of Yorkshire life and lore, J Fairfax-Blakeborough, expressed the opinion that 'our folk-speech, as commonly-used everyday language, is unlikely to survive the next three generations'. He admitted that his prophecy might not apply to remote, isolated parts of the countryside, but he had seen too many dialect terms disappear and too many children of dialect-speaking parents using standard English to be more optimistic.

Life has changed, and is still changing, with such rapidity that terms become obsolete along with the things they described. If very old people refer to a bad headache by saying **'Ah've an 'eead like a set pot'**, it makes sense to them because they remember what a **set pot** (a huge boiler) looked like. But this and other wash-day items such as **posser, piggin** and **voider** have been banished by the modern washing machine. Stanley Ellis, one of the pioneer field-workers involved in the *Survey of English Dialects*, has commented that many of the farming items whose dialect names he so laboriously recorded no longer have any place in modern agriculture.

Yet, whilst it is true that many dialect words have become the linguistic artefacts of a bygone age, there is so much left that is viable and wonderfully expressive, even in the context of contemporary society. With a considerable number of people retaining a smattering of dialect, and an enthusiastic remnant of fluent speakers, there is still the possibility of keeping this language alive. The survival of 'broad Yorkshire' is to some extent up to us. If we do not use it, we shall lose it.

Pronunciation and Spelling

The way Yorkshire people speak is constantly being misunderstood and misrepresented, especially on radio, television and in films. With certain exceptions, such as the refreshingly authentic Barnsley speech which we were treated to in the film *Kes*, it seems to be assumed that any actor or actress can imitate 'broad Yorkshire' – or, for that matter, broad Lancastrian or any of the northern forms of speech. In the worst cases, all such actors do is broaden the vowels – though rarely with consistency – and speak either in a laboured drawl suggestive of slow-wittedness, or in the brusque and brutal monosyllables associated with 'trouble at t' mill'.

From commercials to serious plays casting is sometimes made with so little regard for authenticity that what are supposed to be Yorkshire people come across as false, strained and unconvincing, mere caricatures speaking what could be called 'bogus northern'. The fact that even the most atrocious imitations of northern accents have not stood in the way of the perpetrators receiving national acclaim for their performance, shows that there is still remarkable ignorance about the nature of regional speech.

There is also a tendency to blur distinctions and assume that all Yorkshire speech is the same. The excellent *Herriot* series, for example, included some good Yorkshire dialect, but the actors came from various parts of the county, and we heard very little of the dialect of Wensleydale and North Yorkshire, where the series is supposed to be set. Conversely, in another famous television series, *Coronation Street*, which is supposed to be set in Lancashire, some of the best performances come from those who have strayed over the Pennines from the West Riding.

The subtleties of a 'broad Yorkshire' accent – the formation of consonants and vowels, the timing, and in particular the intonation – are not easily imitated by someone from outside the region. A Londoner, for example, can usually manage the flat vowels in words like 'man' or 'bus', but sooner or later we hear an uncharacteristic diphthong, or the first part of **summat** pronounced as if it were standard English 'some', or the lengthening of 'a' in words like 'last', 'after' and 'bath'. As with any 'foreign language' the only way to establish what it sounds like is to listen attentively to native speakers, either in everyday life or in recordings such as those mentioned in the bibliography. Ideally, all the examples and extracts contained in this book should be heard rather than seen.

The mere printed word cannot do justice to the sounds of Yorkshire dialect, and there is always the risk that however faithfully the words are spelt they will be mispronounced. For example, because **nowt** contains the same letters as 'now', people assume that the pronunciation is 'now' with a 't' added. In most parts of Yorkshire, however, the pronunciation of this common word is more like 'naw-oot'.

In spite of these limitations we can in this chapter give some account of the basic sounds of Yorkshire dialect, and explain the major differences between the West Riding pronunciation and that of the North and East Ridings.

'Broad' vowels are pure vowels

The term 'broad' carries with it the idea of something rather crude and unrefined. Yet the vowels used in Yorkshire and in other northern dialects are virtually the same as those heard in French, German, Italian, Spanish – and, indeed, most of the world's languages. It is standard English which is the odd man out – first, with its pronunciation of 'a' in words like 'man', a sound which is as close to 'e' as 'a', and is written in the International Phonetic Alphabet as æ. In contrast, the Yorkshire pronunciation of **man** appears in the IPA not as [mæn], but as [man].

Standard English is also exceptional in its use of diphthongs, that is, two vowels sounded as one syllable. This gives the 'rounded' effect we hear in a word such as 'name' (where an exaggeration of the diphthong could be written as 'nay-eem') or in a word such as 'go' ('go-oo'). In contrast to these rounded forms, Yorkshire dialect tends to use vowels which are pure and free from the additional vowel – though it does have diphthongs of its own.

Vowels in detail

a as in **brass**, is usually short, even in words where there is a longer 'a' in standard English – 'bath', 'laugh', 'grass', etc. A good example of this is **fatther**, where an extra 't' is usually included to indicate the shortened vowel.

In older dialect-speakers in certain areas this sound is kept after the 'w' in words such as the following, where standard English has an 'o' sound: **want, what, swan, wasp** etc.

ah can also be used to spell the short vowel, as in the Yorkshire equivalent of 'I', for example: **Ah knaw . . . Ah'm stalled . . . Did Ah?**

ah is the usual way of writing the longer vowel we have in standard English words like 'cart', 'yard' etc. We meet this in WR dialect words such as **abaht, claht, tahn** etc.

ah is also used to show this vowel in words where we might expect an 'aw' sound. For example: **wahr** (war), **wahrm** (warm), the latter pronounced to rhyme with 'harm'.

e may be short, as in 'bed', or sometimes long as in 'name', though there are regional variations in this longer vowel.

ee is the sound of standard English 'feel', but in Yorkshire dialect it can become the diphthong **ee-a**, as in **'eead** (head).

i is short, as in 'bit', or may be used to write the vowel in 'bite'. However, as this is a flatter sound in certain areas, some writers use spellings such as **tahme** for 'time', **fahve** for 'five' etc.

o may be short, as in 'pot', and there is a growing use of a long, unrounded 'o' in words such as **stone**, where in earlier dialect a diphthong was used (see overleaf).

aw is a common sound in Yorkshire dialect, often replacing the long 'o' of standard English in words such as 'know', which becomes **knaw**.

u When short this is never pronounced as in standard English 'cut', 'nut', 'shut' etc, but as in 'put' – the same vowel as in 'foot'.

oo usually spells the longer 'u' form in such words as 'gloom' and 'room'. Note that this sound is always long in the dialect, whereas some English speakers shorten it in words like 'room', 'book' and 'look'.

Certain other vowels are not quite what they appear. The 'ir' sound in words like **first**, for example, is much shorter, so that it sounds like '**fust**' or '**fost**', which is how it is sometimes written.

NB The word 'Yorkshire' itself is regularly mispronounced. The vowel in the second part is not 'ear' (Yorkshear) or 'ire' (as in 'fire'), but 'er' (as in 'teacher'), which is why in the dialect it is usually spelt **Yorksher.**

Diphthongs

As has been pointed out, though Yorkshire does not use the 'posh' rounded vowels of standard English, it does have diphthongs of its own.

aa similar to the sound of standard English 'air' occurs in words like **naame**, roughly the equivalent of 'nay-em'. This is especially important in North and East Riding dialect. A similar diphthong is used in WR, especially in the Huddersfield and Holmfirth areas, where **dahn** (down) is pronounced 'day-en', **tahn** (town) 'tay-en' etc, with the same vowel in words such as **meyas** (mouse).

ooa in words like **flooar, dooar, afooare** – roughly the equivalent of 'oo-er' – and in earlier dialect in words like **stooane, rooad** etc.

ow in words like **browt, owt** and **nowt** is in most areas not like the sound of the standard English spelling (eg cow) but more like 'aw-oo'. This sound is also used in South Yorkshire in words where a long 'o' would normally be used.

oi in WR words like **coit, throit, 'oil.**

eea in words like **ageean, deeath, streeat.**

ei, ey in WR words like **reight, feight, speyk.**

ew in WR words like **new, blue, music** etc, sometimes written **neew, bleeue** or **blew, meeusic** or **mewsic** etc. This ancient sound, still used in certain parts of Yorkshire, is very similar to the Celtic vowel used by the Welsh, a diphthong formed of 'ee' and 'ew'. A similar sound appears in NR words such as **leuk** (look), **beuk** (book) etc.

Triphthongs

These are three vowels pronounced as one syllable, and are mostly given their full value in Yorkshire dialect. For example, words like 'fire' (fah-ee-er) are never slurred and reduced to a single vowel (far) – as in the case of certain speakers of English. However, in WR one or two triphthongs are reduced to a single vowel: **flahr** (flower), **shahr** (shower) etc.

Consonants

These are as in standard English, though pronounced more emphatically. For example, in some parts of Yorkshire the final 'd' is emphasised by the addition of a very brief vowel, so that **lad**, for example, can sound almost like 'ladd(er)'. This can apply to other consonants especially at the end of a phrase, when emphasis is needed, eg **ther wor nobbut fifty-three(yer).**

Though the consonant 'h' sometimes appears in spelling, it is rarely sounded, exceptions being, curiously enough, mild curses such as **What the hummer!** Yorkshire people drop all their 'h's, not through slackness, but as a matter of policy – just as happens in French and Italian. An apostrophe is normally used to show where the 'h' once was, mainly to avoid confusion.

Subtle differences occur in the pronunciation of certain standard consonants. Final 's', for example, is not always pronounced unvoiced ('ss') but sometimes in the voiced form, sounding like 'z'. Whereas standard English speakers usually say 'he saw us' (uss), Yorkshire dialect speakers would invariably say **'e saw us** (uz). This tendency to use the voiced form is also seen in 'but' which is usually **bud.**

Final 'g' in the 'ing' sound is almost always absent in Yorkshire dialect. For example: **laikin', shahtin', fettlin', flippin'**. The 'ng' sound within a word does not have the 'g' pronounced, as it is, for example, in standard English 'finger' (fing-ger). In Yorkshire dialect such words as **finger** are parallel to 'singer', where the 'g' is not sounded.

The glottal stop

This is natural to a speaker of Yorkshire dialect, but very difficult for standard English speakers to imitate. I once had the greatest difficulty, during the production of a radio play, in getting a London actor, taking the part of a Yorkshireman, to pronounce phrases like **in t' cave**! He persisted in saying 'in cave'. Then he tried to get the effect of the glottal stop by counting a second or two between the words – 'in . . . cave'. This was even worse, so we settled for 'int cave', which tended to sound like 'inter cave'. In reality the 't' is not actually sounded, but is replaced by a brisk opening and shutting of the glottis at the top of the windpipe.

Sometimes the glottal stop is used instead of 't' within a word, as well as in place of 'the'. For example, **get it etten** (eaten), **gerr it etten** or, with glottal stops, **ge' i' e'en**.

Contractions

The tendency to run separate words together into a smoothly-pronounced phrase is common in Yorkshire dialect, and gives a comical effect when written down in this way. For example:

Worriwiissen? Was he alone?
Weerstabin? Where have you been?
Lerrergerritersen Let her get it herself
Astagorriwithi? Have you got it with you?
Yamtadni I haven't had any
Thamunsupupanshurrup You must drink up and be quiet

It has become fashionable to print this kind of 'comic' Yorkshire, but it is usually slang rather than dialect, and the artificial contractions make the phrases look more bizarre than they are in reality.

The branches of Yorkshire dialect

Most of the sounds of 'broad Yorkshire' are common to all three main dialect branches, but there is a major difference in the way certain vowels and diphthongs are pronounced in West Riding dialect on the one hand, and in the North and East Riding dialects on the other. This can be summarised as follows:

	Standard English	West Riding	North and East Riding
(a)	about	**abaht**	**aboot**
	down	**dahn**	**doon**
	house	**'ahse**	**'oose**
	out	**aht**	**oot**
	mouse	**mahse**	**moos**
	round	**rahnd**	**roond**
	south	**sahth**	**sooth**

This is the most striking of the differences, and the

pronunciation is always clear from the spelling.

(b)	boot	**booit**	**beeat**
	fool	**fooil**	**feeal**
	goose	**gooise**	**geeas**
	soon	**sooin**	**seean**
	school	**schooil**	**skeeal**

Some NR and ER words have this diphthong where WR has a single vowel, eg **deea** (do), **leeak** (look), or where WR has a different diphthong. In addition, in the north-western part of the NR we have **feul, seun, skeul** etc.

(c)	don't	**dooant**	**deeant**
	door	**dooar**	**deear**
	floor	**flooar**	**fleear**
	home	**'ooam**	**'eeam**
	nobody	**nooabody**	**neeabody**

Note that NR speakers tend to use the WR forms of **dooar**, **flooar** etc, and in NER there are three ways of saying 'home': **'ooam, 'eeam** and **yam**.

(d)	speak	**speyk**	**speeak**
	peas	**peys**	**peeas**
	teach	**teych**	**teeach**
	preach	**preych**	**preeach**
(e)	coal	**coil**	**cooal**
	coat	**coit**	**cooat**
	foal	**foil**	**fooal**
	hole	**'oil**	**'ooal**
	throat	**throit**	**throoat**

These are by no means the only differences in vowels. Take, for example, such a common word as 'father'. In the WR this is usually **fatther**, but in NER **feyther** or **faather**.

There are other less obvious differences in the pronunciation of certain consonants. In WR, 'r' is sometimes rolled, whereas in NER it is more like a West Country 'r' and pronounced in words like **dark, farmer, fower** (four), **yakker** (acre) etc.

Before 'r', speakers from Cleveland and East Yorkshire tend to soften 'd' and 't'. For example, 'dry' becomes **dthry,** 'country' becomes **counthry**, 'stranger' becomes **sthranger** etc.

South Yorkshire, too, has its own subtle variations in sound. As a boy I was puzzled by the fact that a school friend always pronounced words like 'started' not with an 'id' at the end, as Bradford folk did, but with a sound like 'e(r)d'. Then I discovered he had spent his early years just to the south, in Halifax. From here southwards the final 'ed' is usually pronounced in this way, and 'boxes', for example, sounds like 'box*ers*'. Then in the Sheffield area, for example, the 'i' sound is more like '**oi**', which is how it is sometimes written. For example: **foive** (five), **loike** (like), **toime** (time), **knoife** (knife) etc.

Variations in spelling

There is no officially-accepted way of writing Yorkshire dialect. Individual ways of attempting to give the phonetic value of a word have produced a variety which causes confusion and is not always accurate.

For example, the WR way of saying 'about' has variously been rendered as **abaht, abaght, abaat** and **abart**. The first is fortunately by far the commonest, and should be encouraged. The last is quite misleading as it may give the impression that the 'r' is pronounced.

Some dialect writers find the use of the apostrophe irksome, but it is a necessary evil in those words where its omission might lead to confusion. For example **'oil** tells us that the word is not 'oil' but **hoil** (hole). The use of the apostrophe falls into four categories:

(a) where an 'h' is dropped – **'e 'as 'ad** (he has had)
(b) where a final 'g' is dropped – **runnin', suppin'**

(c) where there is a glottal stop – **t' gaffer, t' match**
(d) where other consonants or vowels are omitted – **'at** (that)
  o' (of) **s'll** (shall) **'em** (them) etc.

A generally-accepted convention is that when the vowel is short the consonant which follows it is doubled.

> **ovver** – 'o' pronounced as in 'not'
> **finnd** – 'i' pronounced as in 'fit'
> **watter** – 'a' pronounced as in 'cat'

One of the most unfortunate tendencies of dialect writers is to alter the spelling of ordinary words, even when they are pronounced more or less the same as in standard English. For example, we occasionally find such unnecessary spellings as the following, written in this rather silly way in order to indicate that dialect is being spoken: **cud** (could), **dookk** (duck), **joost** (just), **luv** (love), **oop** (up), **sed** (said), **wimmin** (women), **wot** (what), **woz** (was) etc.

As a general rule I suggest that Yorkshire dialect should be written with the normal standard English spelling in those words where there is no difference in pronunciation other than the use of broad vowels.

Standardised spelling

There is little likelihood that a standard system of writing Yorkshire dialect will be universally accepted, mainly because writers will incline to their individual preferences in spelling. In any case, a great variety exists in the dialect that has already appeared in print, and if we are to read it we have to be prepared to cope with wide variations in spelling.

Even so, the system used in this book (apart from extracts of early material) is offered as a basis for standardised spelling. I have based it on the best of the traditional way of writing Yorkshire dialect, showing distinctive sounds as clearly as possible and rationalising the worst inconsistencies.

In order to reduce the number of apostrophes – which seem to be sprinkled all over Yorkshire dialect like confetti – I have not used an apostrophe where a final 'g' is missing, or in the case of **wi** (with) or where an initial 'h' can be omitted without ambiguity. In the prose and verse selections I have kept the original spelling, modified here and there for the sake of consistency or clarity.

Verbs and Pronouns

Although Yorkshire dialect has certain irregular verbs, mostly survivals of earlier English, the majority are very simple. Such problems of comprehension as may arise usually come from vocabulary rather than structure.

The present tense

Here are the subject pronouns, with their various spellings, followed by an example of a verb in the present tense.

Ah (or **Aw**)	**Ah sup**	I drink
tha WR, **thoo** NER	**tha knaws**	you know
'e	**'e addles**	he earns
shoo, sher, sh'	**sh' dons**	she puts on
wer, wi	**wi laik**	we play
yer, yo(u)	**yer shift**	you move
they, ther, the'	**the' lig**	they lie

tha, thoo, the singular, familiar form of 'you', is commonly used in Yorkshire dialect as the 'thou' of earlier English.

The pronoun 'she' is pronounced with the same vowel as 'the', not as standard English 'shee'. It is usually written **sher** or **she** in NER, and **shoo** or **shu** in WR. As these two spellings suggest a long 'oo' sound, a better spelling might be **sh'**, with **shoo** for the emphatic form.

NB. The standard way of saying 'I am' is **Ah'm** in WR, but **Ah's** in NER.

Certain verbs have more than one form in the present tense, sometimes because there were alternative forms in the original Scandinavian. For example:

'e wooant	**'e weeant**	he won't
'e maks	**'e meks**	he makes
'e taks	**'e teks**	he takes
'e 'as	**'e 'es**	he has
'as-ta?	**'es-ta?**	have you?
'atta?	**'etta?**	are you?

Interrogatives like the last two examples can be puzzling to non-dialect-speakers. For example:

Dusta-knaw? (or **do'st-ta knaw?**) Do you know?

The present continuous uses part of the verb 'to be':

Ah'm bahn I'm going WR
tha's gannin/gahin you're going NER

The ordinary present tense would be:

'e goas ter t' chapil ivvery Sunda WR
'e gans ti markit ivvery Wedn'sda NER

Unusual forms and uses

A form which remains the same whichever pronoun is used is **mun** (must). Other verbs look strange because letters are omitted. For example **'od** is a shortened form of 'hold', **tonned** is 'turned' etc. Sometimes there are two forms of the same verb. For example, 'I asked him' is either **Ah axed 'im** or **Ah ass'd 'im.**

Several verbs are used in unusual ways, such as **larn** (learn) in the sense of 'teach'. Then there are past participle forms used as the main stem, as in **mind yer dooant loss it** (lose it), **bust it** (break it) etc.

The future tense

In WR dialect the immediate future – something about to happen – is expressed by using this very common verb **bahn.**

the're bahn ter laik at taws
they're going to play marbles

Ah'm bahn ter side them pots
I'm going to put those dishes away

In NER the equivalent of bahn is **off ti:**

'e's off ti shut t' yat
he's going to shut the gate

For the normal, more distant, future **shall** is used, usually reduced to **s'll** or **'ll:**

wi s'll oppen ter-morn
we shall open tomorrow

Ah s'll (or **Ah's**) **nivver gu theeare ageean**
I shall never go there again

The difference between the two kinds of future tense can be illustrated as follows:

Ah'm bahn ter bray yond lad
I'm going to hit that boy

Ah s'll bray 'im if 'e dunt gi'e ower
I shall hit him if he doesn't stop

The past tense

Yorkshire dialect has certain forms of the past tense which at first sight appear to be an ungrammatical use of standard English. For example:

Ah telled 'im WR	**'e tellt 'im ti rist 'issel** NER
I told him	he told him to have a rest

This is, in fact, historically correct, and is simply an earlier non-inflected form of the verb which dialect has preserved (cf modern German *ich erzähle* I tell, *ich erzählte*, I told).

Another survival sometimes met in Yorkshire dialect concerns the verb 'to get'. We still find the form of the past tense **gat** for 'got', commonly used way back in the seventeenth century, eg 'The pains of hell gat hold upon me' (Psalm 116: 3. King James's Version). In this same Authorised Version the past participle of 'to get' is 'gotten'. Whereas this has been reduced to 'got' in standard English, the earlier 'gotten' survives in American English and in Yorkshire dialect – though here the form is more usually **getten**:

'e gat wed	**'e's getten wed**
he got married	he's got married

There are several other examples of how the 'strong' or inflected form of the verb has been preserved: **fahnd, fan** or **fun** (found), **brak** (broke), **spak** (spoke), **ett** (ate) etc, and in NR we occasionally meet forms like **snew** (snowed) and **fraze** (froze).

The past tense of 'to make' is usually pronounced with a short 'e'. For example:

wi med a reight mullock on it
we made a real mess of it

In NER especially we sometimes find what grammarians call a 'weak' form of the verb where we would not expect it:

'e knawed all aboot it	**seea wer comed awaa oot**
he knew all about it	so we came out

Past participles are often very different in Yorkshire dialect, usually because they retain an earlier form:

brokken	broken	**med**	made
browt	brought	**putten**	put
brussen	burst	**riven**	torn
chozzen	chosen	**selled**	sold
etten	eaten	**shakked**	shaken
fergetten	forgotten	**shotten**	shot
flaid	frightened	**shutten**	shut
frozzen	frozen	**spokken**	spoken
fun	found	**ta'en**	taken
getten	got	**telled**	told
gi'en	given	**tenged**	stung
gooan	gone	**tret**	treated
hodden	held	**wed**	married
letten	let	**wokken**	woken

In some cases there is more than one form. As the schoolchild is supposed to have said, '**Ah've gooan an' putten "putten" when Ah owt to ev putten "put"**'. In earlier dialect literature, other unusual past participles can be seen, such as **brust** (burst), **flitten** (moved house), **strucken** (struck), **sitten** (sat), **sprodden** (spread) and **thrussen** (thrust).

A continuous form of the past is similar to that used in standard English. A good example is the first line of the well-known WR song:

> **Wheeare wor ta bahn when Ah saw thee?**
> Where were you going when I saw you?

The conditional

There are two ways of making a past conditional statement in standard English:

> if it had been fine . . .   had it been fine . . .

In Yorkshire dialect there is a tendency to use the second of these forms. For example:

> **'ad 'e been 'ungry 'e'd 'ave etten t' lot**
> if he'd been hungry he'd have eaten it all

The unlikely-looking **mud** is the dialect form of 'might'. This occurs in the common WR phrase:

> **it mud 'a' been wahr**
> it might have been worse

Note also the form **sud** for 'should'.

Negatives

In both WR and NER speech the equivalent of 'not' is usually **nut**, and in WR there is also **nooan**. For example:

> **thoo 'll nut finnd owt**   **Ah'm nooan bahn yonder**
> you 'll not find anything   I'm not going there

The following special forms of the negative should also be noted:

Ah ammot	I'm not
Ah hennot	I haven't
Ah dursn't	I daren't
Ah munt, munnot	I musn't
Ah weeant	I won't

Very common negative expressions are **nowt** (nothing), **nobbut** (only) and '**Nay!**', which is used rather than 'No' when the speaker wants to make an emphatic denial or contradiction. For example:

'Is that t' finish?' 'Nay! It's nobbut just started'

Double negatives, though nowadays grammatically unacceptable in standard English, are common in dialect:

'e nivver did nowt for nooab'dy
he never did anything for anybody

wi 'aven't done nowt wrang
we haven't done anything wrong.

'e nivver said nowt neeaways ti neean on 'em
he never said anything at all to anybody

Ah dooan't want nowt ner mooare	**ner me nawther**
I don't want anything else	nor me either

neeabody's neea reeight ti tak owt oot o' neeabody's gardin
nobody's any right to take anything from anybody's garden.

Reflexive verbs and pronouns
These are more common in dialect than in standard English. A Yorkshireman, for example, does not 'sit down' but 'sits' (originally 'sets') 'himself down'. Hence the common greeting:

Sit thissen dahn, lad! WR   **Sit thissel doon, lass!** NER

Similarly, rather than 'to get washed' we have the form (as in French, German etc) 'to wash oneself'. Here is the conjugation of this verb to show the reflexive pronouns:

Ah wesh missen   **wi wesh wersens**
tha weshes thissen   **yer wesh yersens**
'e weshes 'issen   **the' wesh thersens**
sh' weshes 'ersen

Variations of these pronouns occur, especially the form of 'self', which can be **sel**. So we have for 'myself', 'yourself' etc.

missel, thissel, 'issel, 'ersel, wersels, yersels, thersels.

Sometimes **ussens** occurs instead of **wersens** for 'ourselves' in WR:

wi 'ed ter wesh ussens i' cowd watter
we had to get washed in cold water

A commonly-used reflexive with no simple equivalent in standard English is:

Frame thissen! (Sometimes reduced to **Frame!**)

This is a short way of saying: 'Get yourself organised. Pull yourself together and get on with the job!' etc.

Other examples of reflexive usage are:

Ah've just bethowt missen (or **mi**)
it's just occurred to me

tha mun seeuit thissen
you must please yourself

shift yersens aht o' t' rooad!
move out of the way!

dooant thee fret thissen!
don't worry!

wi mooast owerslept wersens
we nearly overslept

Sitha! (Look!) is also a reflexive verb, being the imperative form 'See thou', and is sometimes written **sither** or **sithee.**

These pronouns, of course, may be used without verbs, as in the following examples:

sh' did it all bi 'ersen   Ah s'll do it missel

Separable verbs

Verbs linked with a preposition, sometimes known as separable, are common in English (to go in, switch off, look up etc). Yorkshire dialect uses many of these and mostly prefers the older separable form to its Latin equivalent. For example, the verb **take off** would be used rather than 'imitate'.

Here are some typical examples:

'e wor takkin 'im off	he was imitating him
deeant tak on seea!	don't make such a fuss!
we'd given thee up	we thought you weren't coming
Ah wish they'd give ovver	I wish they 'd stop
sh' wor sickened off wi it	she was disgusted with it
stop it off!	stop doing it!
dooant thee let on!	don't tell anybody!
tha mun think on!	you must remember!
wait on! or **'od on!**	just wait a minute!

In all such phrases the emphasis must be on the preposition, not on the verb.

Possessives, Plurals and Prepositions

Here are some of the non-verbal grammatical points, not easy to classify, which occur in Yorkshire dialect, and especially in dialect literature.

Possessive adjectives and pronouns

These differ only slightly from standard English:

mi, ma	my	**mine, mahne**	mine
thi, thy	your	**thine**	yours
'is	his	**'is**	his
'er	her	**'ers**	hers
wer, ahr WR **oor** NER	our	**ahrs** WR **oors** NER	ours
yer	your	**yours**	yours
the'r	their	**theirs**	theirs

Sometimes **us** is used for 'our', especially in WR (eg **us dinners** etc).

Note that **thy** rather than **thi** is used for emphasis:

> **it's nut thy brass, tha knaws**
> it's not *your* money, you know

Another emphatic use of the possessive occurs in phrases like:

> **that gurt gob o' thine**
> That big mouth of yours

Omission of possessives

Where standard English would have an apostrophe 's', dialect often gives no indication of the possessive, except by the context. This is especially true of names. For example, written inside a hymn-book belonging to the author's grandfather were the words: **Hiram Kellett book**. In conversation you might hear somebody referred to as **John Willie Smith wife**, or **Albert Sucksmith brother lad**. An example from North Yorkshire quoted by Bill Cowley in *A Cleveland Anthology* is **oor Jack speead** for 'our Jack's spade'.

More rarely this occurs without a name being involved. For example:

it wor in t' maister pooak	**them's mi fatther booits**
it was in the master's bag	those are my father's boots

t' moos lowpt intiv it hooal
the mouse jumped into its hole

Family names

In Yorkshire dialect a possessive is used when a speaker is referring to members of his or her family. It is not enough to say 'John', 'Mary' etc, but:

ahr or **oor John** . . .   **thy Mary**. . .   **their Albert** etc

Plurals

There are a few nouns which have an unusual plural, mostly because they retain the older form:

childer	children
een WR, **ees** NER	eyes
hosen	stockings
shoon, shooin	shoes
fowks, fooaks	people
beeas(t)	cattle
kye NER	cattle
spice	sweets

We also have double plurals:

bellus, bellusses	bellows
gallus, gallusses	braces

Quantities are usually expressed without the plural ending, because it is clear that the plural is involved. For example:

fower inch (four inches), **fahve mahle** (five miles), **six pund** (six pounds), **ten bob** (ten shillings), **fowerteen yakker** (fourteen acres)

In dialect writing we often come across terms from the pre-decimal days such as:

a sovrin	a pound
a guinea	one pound one shilling
three quid, pahnd, pund	three pounds
'awf a crahn (or **croon**)	two shillings and sixpence
a florin	two shillings (twenty-four pence)
a bob	a shilling (twelve old pence)
a tanner	sixpence
a threp'ny bit	a threepenny piece
tuppence	two pence
a hawp'ny ('awp'ny)	a half-pence piece
a farthin	a quarter of a penny

NB A **gill** is half a pint in early dialect literature – and still is to many Yorkshire people.

Plurals are not usually used with periods of time. For example:

three month   **five year sin**   **two week owd**

This does not apply to 'day' or 'night', eg:

fower days   fo'ty neets

Note that **a twelve-month** is often used instead of 'a year'.

The plural is regularly mixed up with the singular. For example:

ther a straange contrary thing, is a woman ER

Numerals

The old system of counting or 'scoring' sheep with special traditional numbers has now only a curiosity value. The form of certain of these numbers possibly goes back to the Celtic of the Ancient Britons, and is similar to what can be seen in Welsh numerals. Here are a few of the systems still in use in the middle of the nineteenth century:

	Swaledale	Wensleydale	Craven	Knares-borough
1	Yahn	Yan	Arn	Yah
2	Tayn	Tean	Tarn	Tiah
3	Tether	Tither	Tethera	Tethera
4	Mether	Mither	Fethera	Methera
5	Mimph	Pip	Pubs	Pip
6	Hithher	Teaser	Aayther	Seezar
7	Lithher	Leaser	Layather	Leezer
8	Anver	Catra	Quoather	Cattera
9	Danver	Horna	Quaather	Horna
10	Dic	Dick	Dugs	Dick
11	Yahndic	Yan-dick	Arnadugs	Yah-dick
12	Tayhndic	Tean-dick	Tarnadugs	Tiah-dick
13	Tetherdic	Tither-dick	Tetheradugs	Tether-a-dick
14	Metherdic	Mither-dick	Fetheradugs	Mether-a-dick
15	Mimphit or Mump	Bumper	Buon	Bumper
16	Yahn-a-mimphit	Yan-a-bum	Arnabuon	Yah-de-bumper
17	Tayn-a-mimphit	Tean-a-bum	Tarnabuon	Tiah-de-bumper
18	Tether-a-mimphit	Tither-a-bum	Tetherabuon	Tether-de-bumper
19	Mether-a-mimphit	Mither-a-bum	Fetherabuon	Mether-de-bumper
20	Jigit	Jigger	Gun-a-gun	Jigger

Note that **yan** (Wensleydale) and **yar** or **yah** (Knares-borough) are still the standard words for 'one' in the North and East Riding dialect areas:

yan o' them lasses   **nobbut a yar pockit**
one of those girls   only one pocket

Two numerical terms common in Yorkshire dialect are **a twoathri** (or **a tuthri**) and **umpteen**, the latter used in standard English, but more common in dialect:

'e oppened a twoathri secks **yon chap's umpteen 'osses**
he opened a few sacks   that man has a lot of horses

Between 'a few' and 'a lot' we have **a good few** or **a fair few**.

With numbers **on** always replaces 'of':

> **ther's three on 'em, umpteen on 'em, a fair few on 'em**

In ER dialect as an alternative to **umpteen** the idea of a large amount can be conveyed by **a vast o'**. For example:

> **ther' wor a vast o' skeeal lads**
> there were a lot of schoolboys

Similarly, in NER the idea of a considerable degree can be conveyed in two other ways:

> **despert lang**   **a desperate good creckiter**
> very long   an exceptionally good cricketer
> **sthrange an' late**
> extremely late ER

With certain numbers the older style of formation is used. This is especially true of times:

> **five an' twenty past** (instead of 'twenty-five past')

Notice also that with times a Yorkshire speaker tends to say, for example, **it's turned three** rather than 'it's just gone three'.

The older way of giving a figure is not restricted to time. In dialect literature we can see it used for age. For example:

> **sh'd lost all 'er teeth afooare sh' wor five an' twenty.**

A common way of saying 'in succession' is, for example:

> **'e went theeare three days 'and-runnin'**

Prepositions

In Yorkshire dialect, many prepositions have a different form or pronunciation, and several are used in special ways. Here they are in alphabetical order:

abaht WR about	**fer** for
aboon above	**fra** WR, **frev** NER from
aboot NER about	**i'** WR **iv** NER in
afooare before	**inter, intul** WR **intiv** NER into
ageean, agen against	**o', ov** of
aht WR out	**on** on; of
ahten out of	**oot** NER out
anent, anenst next to, opposite	**ovver, ower** over
amang NER among	**rahnd** WR round
atween, atwixt between	**roond** NER round
baht WR without	**sin** since
behunt, behint NER behind	**ter, tul** WR **tiv** NER to
bi by	**thru** WR, **thruff** NER through
dahn WR down	**wi** WR **wiv** NER with
doon NER down	**wivoot** NER without

Note that 'opposite' is expressed by **ovver (ower) agen**

An intrusive 'v' occurs in NER before a vowel. Compare **ti markit** with **tiv a** (to a), **wiv a** (with a), **frev a** (from a) etc.

When they occur in front of 'the' or 'it', certain prepositions may be confusing because of the contracted pronunciation. For example **i' t'** (in the) sounds like 'it'. However, the meaning is usually clear in written dialect:

wi t'	**o' t'**	**on 't**	**tul t'**	**bi t'**
with the	of the	of it	to the	by the

Special uses of prepositions

One of the commonest differences is that in dialect **on** is used for 'of'. As already noted, this occurs with numbers, eg **yan on 'em** (one of them).

It may also occur in other places where we might expect 'of'.

For example:

nut 'at Ah knawed on   **gi'e us 'od on it**
not that I knew of   let me have hold of it
     'e could mak mair brass oot on 't
     he could make more money out of it

on does not necessarily mean 'of', and can be used as in standard English (eg **on t' table**). But there may still be some special meaning, as in the phrase **Ah 'd summat on wi 'im**, meaning 'I'd a difficult job, he gave me a lot of trouble' etc.

Sometimes **on** is used alongside **of** or **o'**. It was said of Lady Ann and the Cliffords that she was **'t' last on 'em an' t' best o' t' lot'**.

In WR dialect **on** is used with **dahn** in expressions of disapproval such as:

Ah'm dahn on yon new gaffer
I don't like that new boss
sh's dahn on peys – an' rheeubub, an' all
she's not keen on peas – or rhubarb, either.

Verbs do not always take the preposition that is grammatically acceptable in standard English. For example, in Yorkshire there is a distinction between to **listen to** and **to listen at**. We may say **'e wor listenin' ter t' band**, but a dialect speaker would say **Listen at this!** to make it emphatic or to draw attention to something, as is also the case in the example:

listen at yon bairn roarin
listen to that child crying

Sometimes **ov** or **o'** is used instead of **on**. For example:

'e allus went theeare ov a Sunda
he always went there on Sundays

In the following example we have **ov** used, and also **to** instead of 'for':

'e 'ad tripe to 'is dinner ov a Setterda
he had tripe for his lunch on Saturdays
they'd mutton ti the'r dinners ov a Thursda
they'd mutton for their dinner on Thursdays

Instead of 'from' we often find 'through' is used. For example:

'e comes thru 'eckmondwike
he comes from Heckmondwike

To express 'until' a dialect speaker usually makes use of **while**:

wi s'll 'appen stay while Munda
we shall perhaps stay until Monday
cahr quiet while 'e's finished t'job
keep quiet till he's finished the work

A curious way of saying 'afterwards' is sometimes met in dialect:

t' bairns 'ad rice puddin at after (or **at efter**)
the children had rice pudding afterwards

There is a similar use of **at** in **at t'morn** (in the morning) and **at t'afternooin** (in the afternoon).

Note that **termorn** or **timorn** means 'tomorrow' and that 'tomorrow morning' is sometimes **termorn i' t' morn**. Note also **yesterneet** (last night).

The prepositions **ovver** and **ower** are used in the sense of 'too'. In NER, for example, we might hear:
t' preeacher's sarmon wor ower lang
the preacher's sermon was too long

There is also the expression for 'once', 'at one (particular) time', 'on one occasion': **once ovver** (or **ower**) WR and **yance ower** (NER)

Oddities and Idioms

There are many peculiarities of vocabulary, grammar and idiomatic usage which help to give Yorkshire dialect its distinctive character. Here are some of the most interesting, though not in any order of importance.

Patterns in vocabulary

It is useful to note common differences which occur on a regular basis between standard English and dialect in such groups as the following:

(a) **neet**	night	**leet**	light	**seet**	sight etc
(b) **breead**	bread	**'eead**	head	**deead**	dead etc
(c) **lang**	long	**strang**	strong	**wrang**	wrong etc
(d) **beg**	bag	**regs**	rags	**wesh**	wash etc
(e) **onny**	any	**monny**	many	**chonce**	chance etc
(f) **rist**	rest	**nivver**	never	**riddy**	ready etc
(g) **owd**	old	**cowd**	cold	**gowd**	gold etc

NB See also the differences between WR and NER (pages 29–31) and watch out for ambiguities – such as **teea**, which is 'tea' in WR, but 'toe' in NER, **claht** WR, which can mean 'cloth' or 'hit' etc.

Differences in consonants do not occur in such a regular way, though there is a group characterised by the omission of a consonant:

thunner thunder, **grummle** grumble, **tummle** tumble, **cannle** candle, **rammle** ramble, **thimmle** thimble etc.

This is not the careless dropping of a consonant, but mostly the preservation of an older form. In 'thunder', for example, 'd' has intruded into **thunner** (cf German *Donner*). Sometimes this works the other way round: 'chimney' is in dialect **chimley, chimla** or **chimbley**, and 'mill' is sometimes **miln**.

False friends

Just as French has its *faux amis*, so Yorkshire dialect has a number of words which do not mean what they appear to mean. Here are a few examples:

flags are mostly not to be waved, but to be walked upon
bawl, roar and **yell** are used for 'to weep', especially loudly
gang is nothing more sinister than 'go'
pawse has nothing to do with intervals, but means 'kick'
real describes something outstandingly good, exciting etc
sin is no more deadly than 'since'
reckon can mean 'pretend', or is a rod across the fire
buzzard is not a bird, but a moth
coil has nothing to do with wire, but is 'coal'
shoot in NER is 'shout'
loose or **lowse** is what a school does at home-time.
brat is not necessarily a child, but may be an apron
grand is not the standard English meaning, but is 'excellent'
starved has to do with cold, not hunger
mash has to do with tea, as well as potatoes
house means the living-room as distinct from the kitchen WR
room means the front or best room – or parlour WR
twisters were honest textile workers
bobby-dazzler is not an anti-police device, but something splendid (pronounced with emphasis on the second word)

There are many other misleading words like this, especially the more obscure terms such as, for example, **fluff** and the quite unconnected **fluffin**, so checking in the Pocket Yorkshire Dictionary (pages 131-40) is advisable.

Words favoured in Yorkshire dialect

A number of words which can be found in any dictionary of standard English have a slightly different meaning in Yorkshire dialect, or are used far more frequently. For example:

band is the word mostly used for 'string' or 'rope'
belly is preferred to 'stomach', when 'belly' is meant
idle is more likely to be used than 'lazy'
oft is more common than 'often'

same as is used to mean 'like'
right (**reight, reet**) often replaces 'very'
fresh is used for 'new', especially in **Owt fresh?** (Any news?)
sharp is the preferred term for 'quick'
rive is the word for 'tear'
shuv, shove is used rather than 'push'
shift is used rather than 'move'
rooad is more likely to be used than 'way'
stupid can mean 'stubborn'
yonder is not poetic, but standard for '(over) there'

Special uses of similar 'ordinary' words can be seen in the examples in the rest of this chapter.

Technical terms

Some of the richest dialect vocabulary is found amongst workers who have traditionally clung to their own technical terms. From time to time word-lists of particular trades, from mining to chimney-sweeping, have been published in the YDS *Transactions*. A few more generally known are given below.

Farming retains many dialect terms, in spite of many others having become obsolete through mechanisation. We have, for example, **barfin, braffin** or **barkum** (horse collar), **britchin** (breachband) and other terms for parts of the harness. In sheep-farming, we have words such as **tup** (ram), **gimmer** (female sheep before it lambs), **wether** (castrated lamb), **hogg** (year-old lamb) and **rig-welted** or **cast** (a sheep or other animal on its back and unable to get up). There are terms for pigs, such as **gilt** (young sow), and for cattle, usually called **beeas(t)** or **kye**, including **stots** (bullocks), **stirks** (bullocks or heifers). Cows require **skelbeeases** (divisions in the cowshed) where they might be tied up to a **boskin, boose-stake,** or **rud-stake**. A cow that is **new-noited**, that is, one which has produced a **cawf** (calf) will give **beeastlins** or **bissling** (the first milk), which might be milked into a **piggin** (small bucket). Farming in the past owed a good deal to the **daytals,** labourers paid by the day, who perhaps did **lowkin** or **lukin** (weeding), who **scaled t' muck** or **t' mannishment** (spread the manure), helped at **hay-timin** and harvested the corn into **attocks** (sheaves) and **pikes** (round stacks). The welcome break in the fields is still known as **lowance** or **drinkins**.

Fishermen have a host of technical terms (see YDS *Transactions* 1948 for Staithes, 1966 for Filey, 1984 for the Humber), with a few such as **coble** (pronounced 'cobble') for a fishing-boat, widely known. Steelworkers have their own technical vocabulary (see YDS *Transactions* 1966), as also do miners (*Transactions* 1981), with some terms, such as the South Yorkshireman's **snap** (packed lunch) in general use. It was the textile mills of the industrial West Riding, however, which gave the highest proportion of dialect terms. Words such as **slack** and **slack-set-up** originally referred to belts too slack on the pulleys, which meant that the looms etc worked more slowly. The opposite effect occurred when the belts were tightened, hence the order **Tighten!** (Get a move on! Clear off! etc.) From the fact that a pulley would not revolve unless the **band** (string, rope) was engaged, came the expression **to keep t' band i' t' nick**, ie to keep a friendship etc ticking over. Similarly, to **get t' little pulleys goin'** was to speed something up. Then there were workers such as **bobbin-liggers**, who replaced bobbins on the spinning-machine, **doffers** who took them off when full of yarn, **twisters**, who twisted the warp and weft ready for the loom, **weyvers** (weavers) and so forth.

Domestic terms are important in dialect, though many are no longer used because of the disappearance of such items as **t'breead-fleg** or **creel**, a rack lowered from the ceiling on which **haver-cake** (oat bread) was dried, later washing. Essential for washday was the **set-pot** (a boiler with a fire-grate beneath), later replaced by a **copper**, and a **dolly-tub** or **peggy-tub**, in which clothes were stirred and squeezed with a wooden **dolly** or **peggy**, later a **posser** with a copper head. Then they would be wrung through the **mengle** (mangle) and spread to dry on a hedge in summer or a clothes-horse in winter, hence the term for the latter of **wint'r-'edge**. Before ironing with a **flat-iron**, the clothes would go in a **voider** or wicker basket. Under the large fire there would be an **assen-ook** (ash pan) in the corner a **poit** or **firepoint** (poker), a **skep** for coal (**coils** or **cooals**) and perhaps a **brandrith**, a moveable iron frame which held a **posnit** and other pans over the fire, or a **rannel-bauk** (cross-beam) with a **reckon** attached from which a kettle might be suspended. For stirring food such as porridge there was a wooden stick or spoon known known as a **thible**.

Dialect words derived from the Romany of Yorkshire gypsies include NER **gadge** (man, fellow) and **charver** (mate, lad).

A multipurpose ending

The addition of the word meaning 'hole', and by extension 'place' – **'oil** in WR, **'ooal** in NR and ER – gives us terms such as the following (WR version):

bobby-'oil police-station, **cake-'oil** mouth, **coil-'oil** coal-house, **dooar-'oil** doorway, **'en-'oil** chicken-run, **fish-'oil, chip-'oil** fish shop, **kall-'oil** place where people gather to gossip, **mengle-'oil** mangle-house, **muck-'oil** filthy or untidy place, **pig-'oil** sty.

A **muck-'oil** is sometimes implied by the exclamation **What an 'oil!** There is also the jocular way of telling somebody to shut the door, **Put t' wood i' t' 'oil!**, and sayings such as **abaht as strong as chip-'oil vinegar** and **dahn i' t' cellar-'oil wheeare t' muck slahts on t' winders.**

Curses and expletives

Exclamations and interjections, especially those of annoyance, are common in Yorkshire dialect. All the curses are mild, however, retaining little of the original meaning.

By gum! and **By gow!** (or **Bi gum!** and **Bi gow!**) are both probably euphemisms for 'by God!' – though it has been suggested that **gum** is a corruption of **gaum** (common sense).

But in dialect the meaning is more like 'Good Lord!', 'My word!', 'Fancy that!' etc. There is also the exclamation **Lors!** (presumably a corruption of Lord!) and the more common **By lad!**, which may perhaps be explained by **t' Owd Lad**, a euphemism for the Devil.

By heck! (or **'eck!**) was originally 'by hell!', but the meaning is milder, and the exclamation **Oh, heck!** is more like 'Oh,dear!'.

Hummer! (or **'ummer!**) is a similar euphemism for 'hell', and is used to express surprise or annoyance in the phrases **By hummer!** and **What the hummer!**:

> **What the 'ummer 'as 'e oppened t' dooar fo'?**
> Why on earth has he opened the door?

Notice that **hummer** is preceded by **the**, not **t'**. The same applies to another substitution for 'hell' in the phrase **Hengments!** (or **'engments!**) or **What the hengments!**.

A curious ER exclamation of this kind is **Bon!**, possibly originating from 'burn ' (in hell). In Walter Turner's tales we have, for example:

> **Bon! Ah'll get wed, Ah will, Ah seer!**
> Dash it all! I'll get married, I really will

As there are several mild curses beginning with **By . . .**, including the less common **By shots!** WR, there has arisen the curious habit in Yorkshire dialect of using **By!** on its own. For example:

> **By! Tha's gooan an' supped t' lot!**
> I say! You've drunk it all.

Deng it! is a softened form of 'Damn it!', and the adjective **denged** the equivalent of 'damned'. Other euphemisms for 'damned', or some similar term of condemnation, are **blamed, blessed, flippin** etc. Instead of saying, 'Well I'll be damned!' a dialect speaker is more likely to say **Well, Ah'll be blowed!**

The verb **drat** is more commonly used than in standard

English, giving the adjective **dratted**, an imprecation like 'damned', and phrases such as **Drat t' politicians!**', the equivalent of 'I don't care a damn about the politicians' etc.

Greetings and imperatives

A form of welcome once commonly used all over Yorkshire, and still to be heard, especially in NER is:

Come thi ways in!   (cf **Come on in!** WR)

The commonest form of greeting in WR is probably the equivalent of 'Now, then', which has at least four different meanings according to the tone used and whether the 'now' is **nah** or the shorter **na**:

1.	*Nah* **then?**	Hello! How are things? etc
2.	*Nah* **then!**	Here we are! Look at this etc
3.	**Na** *then,* **lad?!**	How are you, then? All right etc
4.	**Na** *then!*	Watch it! That's enough! etc

A greeting in the WR area can be no more than **Na, lad!** but it is still a genuine enquiry meaning: 'Now, then. How are you, friend?' Note also **'Ah do?, 'Ow do?** (How are you?).

Imperatives, or commands, include the following:

Ey up!	Look out!
'Od thi wisht!	Be quiet!
'Od thi din!	Shut up!
Look (or **mak**) **sharp!**	Be quick!
Ger agate! WR **Gang agaate!** NER	Get a move on!
Tighten! or **Tak thi 'ook!**	Clear off!
Aht o' t' rooad!	Out of the way!
Get shut on 't!	Get rid of it!
Less of thi owd buck!	Don't be cheeky!
Tak nooa gaum on it!	Don't take any notice!

In addition, there are such imperatives as **Sitha!, Frame!, Wait on!** etc, already mentioned (pp 40-41).

A delightful way of saying goodbye in Yorkshire dialect is the exhortation to virtuous behaviour:

Na *then*, lad – Bi good!

Expressions of disbelief, surprise and protest

When a Yorkshire listener does not accept what is being said, or is taken aback by it, there is a choice of expressions to convey this:

Give ovver! or **Gi'e ower!, Ger away wi yer!, Ger 'ooam!** and the curious variation on the latter **Well, Ah'll gu to ahr 'ahse!**

As a cry of protest, meaning 'not at all, on the contrary' etc, there is the use of **nay!**, which is much stronger than **no** or **nooa**. For example:

theeare's John Willie! Nay! It's John Willie brother
there's John Willie! No, it isn't! It's John Willie's brother

A common way of giving someone a mild though friendly rebuke is to pull them up with:

Nay, *lad*! or **Nay, *lass*!**

Here the emphasis is on the second word, otherwise the phrase is just a simple denial. An expression of regret heard in my boyhood, but never these days, was the expressive **Nay! The shames!**

The use of *Aye*

Although 'yes' can be used in Yorkshire dialect the standard affirmative is **Aye** (pronounced 'eye').

Aye is also used as an interrogative, and when said very slowly, in a drawled rising tone, it has the equivalent of 'Is that really true? Well, I am surprised!' etc.

'Sh's 'ad two 'usbands afooare, tha knaws'
'Aye?!' (about two seconds duration!)

The emphatic use of *that*

Very characteristic of Yorkshire speech is the use of **that** to emphasise a previous statement. For example:

> **'e's a champion cricketer, 'e is** *that*!
> he's an excellent cricketer, he really is

Then there is the use of **that** in the sense of 'so':

> **wi wor that 'ungry wi could 'ave etten owt**
> we were so hungry we could have eaten anything

Phrases tagged on

Other words and phrases are often tagged on to a statement. These include **like, 'e does** etc, **an' all** (as well) and **an' then**. The latter is really short for **an' then Ah'll see**, as in the anecdote about the man who told the waiter each time he brought a Yorkshire pudding: **'Ah'll 'ave another, 'an then. . .'** When asked by the waiter, 'And then what, sir?', he replied **'an' then mak 'em a bit thicker.'**

The verb *to hear that*

In Yorkshire we do not simply 'hear' something, but hear it told, so the equivalent verb is **hear tell**. When **that** is not used to mean 'so' it is usually reduced to **'at**:

> **Ah 'eeard tell 'at sh'd flitted ter Brid**
> I heard she'd removed to Bridlington

Demonstrative adjectives: *this, these, them.*

When **this/these, them** (those) are used in dialect it is usually with **'ere** or **theeare** added, eg **this 'ere dooar, that theeare tree, these 'ere pigs, them theeare 'osses** etc.

Very common is the use of **yond** or **yon** for 'that' or 'those':

> **yon cauves mun gu i' yon mistal**
> those calves must go in that cowshed

The use of *fair* and *–ish*

In front of an adjective **fair** means 'really, to a considerable extent'. For example, **'e wor fair flummoxed** (absolutely bewildered). This is similar to the use of **reight/reet** (very) but is more emphatic:

Ah wor fair starved (I really was cold).

The expression **reight/reet fair** means something like 'you surely agree with this':

reight fair, yon side can't laik football
you must admit, that team can't play football

Characteristic of ER is the addition of **-ish** giving **fairish** (considerable, considerably) and such adjectives as **shortish, smartish, baddish, queerish** etc.

Not being able to bear something or somebody

There are two ways of expressing this:

Ah cannot (a)bide yond woman
I can't stand that woman
sh' cannot do wi bein moithered
she can't bear to be flustered

The two senses of *cap*

The verb **cap** can be used in the sens of 'to surprise', eg **Ah wor fair capped**. There is also the adjective **cappin** (surprising, astonishing):

There is, in addition, the sense of 'to beat, surpass':

it caps owt   it beats anything

Feeling cold

A Yorkshire person who is feeling cold may declare that he or she is **nithered, frozzen ter deeath** and especially **starved**:

wi wor fair starved aht theeare
we were really cold out there

A person who easily feels the cold may be described as **nesh**, or be treated to the comment: **Ee, tha's a starved-un!**

Weather expressions

Heavy rain can be described in several ways – **teemin, tipplin (dahn, doon), chuckin it dahn, peshin it dahn, silin dahn** etc, and when it starts to rain it is said that **it's comin on.**

Breezy weather may be described as **fresh**, cold weather as **parky**, and when there is a covering of snow it is said to be **white ovver/ower.** In NR especially when a blizzard or blown snow makes it difficult to see ahead it is said that it is **stowerin**.

When the weather improves it is said to **take** or **get up.**

Uses of *back*

Though grammatically incorrect because it is tautologous (saying the same thing twice) the verb **back back** is used:

ther's nowt else for it; we mun back back
there's nothing else we can do but reverse

There is also **back'ards**, the opposite of **forr'ard**, sometimes in the form **back'ards rooad.**

A reasonably polite term for 'posterior' (and even **arse** is less vulgar in dialect) is **back-side** – not to be confused with **back-end**, which refers to the autumn:

wi s'll come an' see thi a' t' back-end
we'll come and see you in autumn

When a Yorkshire person cancels an appointment this is invariably described as to **give back-word.**

Uses of *job*

As in standard English this can mean employment, a piece of work etc, and satisfaction or relief can be expressed by **It's a good job!**

In dialect, however, **job** on its own is often used in the sense of 'a bad job', something to be regretted or deplored:

By gum! Yond garden's a job!

The implication is that the garden is in a mess and will need lots of work. However, the term is sometimes used to describe people:

'e's a job, is yond!

Here the idea is that the person referred to is so useless, unreliable or otherwise deficient that there is no hope of improvement.

Similar expressions of regret are **It's a job!** and **Ah'll 'ave a job ter finish it afooare Sunda'**, the latter usage more common in dialect than standard English.

A curious use of **job**, really a kind of understatement, is when it refers to an operation, or perhaps having a baby, hence:

wi can't come on accahnt of ahr Rachel's job

The fact is that **job** is widely used in Yorkshire dialect, and means more than 'work'. For example, somebody asking what has happened, say, if a family dispute has arisen, might enquire: **What's all this job, then?**

Uses of *sooart*

Note these various ways of using **sooart**:

nowt o' t' sooart	**t' fust o' t' sooart**
nothing of the kind	the first of its kind.

It is also used of people:

'e's nut t' sooart 'at 'ould lend owt
he's not the kind of person to lend anything
sh's a reight gooid sooart, is Edith
she's a really kind person, is Edith

A Yorkshire person not feeling well may say of himself **Ah'm a bit aht/oot o' sooarts.**

Expressions concerning health

Ask Yorkshire people how they are, and you may get one of the following replies – given here in order of desirability:

champion!	everything is perfect
grand!	feeling really well
nicely	quite well
nobbut middlin	only average
fair ter middlin	not at my best
just fair	not all that well
nobbut dowly	feeling miserable, poorly
badly	very ill
failin	seriously ill, getting worse
goin' dahn t' nick	not going to get better

The worst that can be said of anybody in respect of health is that a person has **getten ter t' far end** (near to death), **looks yonderly** (faraway look in the eyes) or **it's aboot owered** (near the end). There is also the ER comment on somebody who looks ill: **'e leeaks a bad leeak**, and the WR equivalent: **Ee! 'e looks a poor object!** (This reduction of a person to a thing also occurs when somebody who is detested is be referred to as **yond article**.)

Whether a person is afflicted by **lugwark, bellywark, teeathwark** or whether he's been **smittled** (WR) or **takken smit** (NER) and caught an infectious disease – or has something more serious, there is always the hope of recovery, expressed by:

Ah'm mendin, on t' mend (better than I was)

Ah'll clog ageean (I'll make a good recovery)

The last expression refers to the cobbler's opinion that a pair of clogs could be repaired yet again, hence the exhortation: **Keep cloggin' on!** (keep going). The opposite would be if somebody died and **popped 'is clogs**.

Terms for left-handedness

Yorkshire dialect has more terms for this than anything else. Typical are **cack-'anded, gallock-'anded** and **cuddy-wifted**, with terms for left-handed people such as **gallocker** and **cuddy-wifter.**

For the distribution of the many variations see map (p184) in H Orton, N Wright *Word Geography of England* (1974).

A term of mild (self) rebuke

The verb to **doit** (dote) is used in WR to describe the forgetfulness, getting confused, slipping up in some way, that is associated with old age. So a person may say of himself/herself:

Ah mun bi doitin'! Ah've getten t' wrong number

Or we might jokingly say to somebody who has forgotten something, got mixed up with dates and so forth (though not all Yorkshire folk would see it as a joke!), **Nay, lad! Tha's doitin!**

A term of endearment

A lovely word, which some of us remember with affection as one addressed to us as children, is WR **doy**, the equivalent of 'dear' or 'darling':

Nah then, doy. 'Ere's a feew spice fo' thi!

Miscellaneous

Phrases which have a special idiomatic meaning, and could be misunderstood, include the following:

Is 'e fooarced ter be theeare?	Is it certain he'll be there?
'e belongs Pocklington	he comes from Pocklington
'e belongs t'mill	he owns the mill
Nay, Ah didn't awn (own) yer	Oh, I didn't recognise you
sh' awned 'ersen i' t' wreng	she admitted she was wrong
allus at t' last push up	always at the last minute
Ah couldn't fashion ter tak it	I couldn't bring myself to, etc
nobbut a mention	just a small amount
it's nut jannock	it's not fair, right etc
Ah s'll gi'e thi what fo'	I'll give you a good hiding
all of a fullock	in a big rush
sam 'od on it!	grab hold of it!
Ah unbethowt missen	I thought better of it
choose 'ow tha does it	no matter how you do it
for all 'e wor clever	in spite of his being clever
sh' fotched/landed 'im a claht	she gave him a clout
Ah'd as lief lig i' bed	I'd just as soon stay in bed
'e wor 'ard on	he was fast asleep
livin tally, ower t'brush	not married but living together
Ah reckon nowt to it	I don't think much of it
Ah can't reckon it up	I don't understand it
it caps owt, Ah seer	it beats anything, it really does
yer tek a good likeness	you're very photogenic
'e's happened an accident	he's had an accident
all ovver t' shop	all over the place
tha's all dothered up	you're covered in mud etc
Ah'm fast for a bit o' band	I'm short of a bit of string
ther's nobbut one apiece	there's only one each
Well, if 'e didn't dee!	Would you believe it? He died
Ah can't thoil it	I don't think its worth spending the money on it

Yorkshire Sayings and Traditions

This chapter brings together classic dialect sayings, traditions and verses, which help to form a picture of the attitude to life of the typical Tyke, as a Yorkshireman is often called.

A Yorkshireman's motto

The best-known statement of Yorkshire philosophy is a kind of traditional motto, usually given in WR dialect. This represents a Tyke's ability to laugh at himself, and especially at his image – not entirely undeserved – as a man of few words, careful with his money to the point of stinginess, rather like his fellow Northerners, the Scots:

> 'Ear all, see all, say nowt;
> Eyt all, sup all, pay nowt;
> An' if ivver tha does owt for nowt –
> Do it fer thissen!

A more serious motto, which gives us a better image, goes:

> Wi mense (decency) tak what's yer awn,
> Wi pluck 'od what's yer awn,
> An' mak that fet (sufficient);
> Gi'e wi oppen 'and –
> But nivver let friendship spoil a bargin.

The Yorkshireman's Coat of Arms

The view of Yorkshire men traditionally taken by the rest of the country is not flattering. In the eighteenth century, for example, we find the first mention of the satirical coat of arms, said to contain a fly, a flea, a magpie and a flitch of bacon, with the following explanation:

A fly will tipple with anybody, so will a Yorkshireman;
a flea will bite anybody, so will a Yorkshireman;
a magpie will chatter with anybody, so will a Yorkshireman;
and a flitch of bacon is never good for anything till it
has been hanged up, no more is a Yorkshireman.

In another version of the coat of arms (see p 68) the bacon is replaced by a gammon of the ham for which Yorkshire was famous, and a horse reminds us of Yorkshire's long association with horse-breeding and trading. John Hartley in his *Seets i' Lundun* remarks that Londoners could hardly believe he was a Yorkshireman, as he wasn't leading a horse.

A Yorkshire toast

The Yorkshireman's reputation for looking after his own interests is neatly summed up in this satirical toast:

> 'Ere's tiv us – all on us – an me an all!
> May wi nivver want nowt, nooan on us –
> Ner me nawther!

An East Riding version of this toast goes:

> 'Ere's tiv us – all on us,
> All on us ivver;
> May neean on us want nowt,
> Neean on us nivver.

There is also the variation:

> 'Ere's ti ye an me,
> An' ti mah wife's 'usband,
> Nut forgettin missen.

A Yorkshireman's grace

Before a meal there is the traditional WR grace:

> God bless us all, an' mak us able
> Ta eyt all t' stuff 'at's on this table

To follow an ungenerous meal there is the satirical verse:

We thank the Lord for what we've getten:
Bud if mooare 'ad been cutten
Ther' d mooare 'a' been etten

Proverbial sayings

The advice to grasp at an opportunity and make the most of it, seen in sayings previously quoted, is summed up in the old Yorkshire proverb:

Cop 'od an stick!   Take hold and hang on!

A realistic appraisal of the necessity for the smoke-blackened mill towns and grimy mines of the West Riding takes us back to the days of the Industrial Revolution:

wheeare ther's muck ther's brass

The poverty experienced by past generations – those not **weel hefted wi brass** – is represented in various Yorkshire sayings. For example, the fact that a joint of meat was expensive, with very little to go round, meant that the family was persuaded to eat as much Yorkshire pudding as possible – this traditionally being served as a first course with gravy, often onion gravy. The idea was simply that those who had their fill of Yorkshire pudding would not have much appetite for the meat which followed. So it could safely be said:

them 'at eyts mooast puddin' gets mooast meyt

The diet of the poor included plenty of herring, a fact reflected in the odd little saying once heard by the author:

T' finest 'errin 'at ivver spak
Said 'Wahrm mi belly afooare mi back!'

The importance of an adequate amount of food for working people is stressed in the WR proverb:

strength goes in at t' mahth

The satirical 'Yorkshireman's Coat of Arms'

This drawing by Peter Kearney is based on the earliest known designs, the first of which was by Thomas Tegg of Cheapside, London (1818) who added the following explanatory verse:

A magpie behold, and a fly and a flea,
And a Yorkshireman's qualifications you'll see,
To backbite and sponge and to chatter amain,
Or anything else, Sir, by which he can gain,
The horse shows they buy few, though many they steal,
Unhang'd they're worth nought, does the gammon reveal.
But let censure stand by and not bias the mind,
For many as bad as the Yorker you'll find.

A later version of this in WR dialect ran as follows:
A flea, a fly, a magpie an' a bacon flitch
Is t' Yorksherman's coit of arms;
An' t' reason they've chozzen theease things sooa rich,
Is 'cos they hev all special charms;
A flea will bite 'ooivver it can –
An' sooa, mi lads, will a Yorksherman!
A fly 'll sup wi Dick, Tom or Dan –
An' sooa, bi gow, will a Yorksherman!
A magpie can talk fer a terrible span –
An' sooa an' all can a Yorsherman!
A flitch is nooa good while it's hung, yer'll agree –
An' nooa mooare is a Yorksherman, dooan't yer see?

Ingratitude and neglecting to repay a kindness is summarised in the WR observation:

etten jock's sooin fergetten   Food that's eaten is soon
forgotten

Of a man too fond of drink it can be said:

e's double-fisted an' threpple-throited (three throats)

A woman who talks at length, including every single detail in her narration, might receive the description:

sh' telled t' tale from t' thread ter t' needle

When somebody makes a good point that is accepted by the listener, the latter may say:

it's weel spokken an' weel ta'en

Of a person who talks for the sake of talking it can be said:

'e talks an' says nowt . . . 'e's said nowt when 'e's done

Critical comments appear in a variety of forms. For example:

tha's same as a man made o' band
you're just like a man made of string

The person so described is ineffectual, useless, the sort of person who would produce an inferior piece of work or **a band-end job**.

Clogs with irons underneath (to raise them above the mud) called **pattens** provided this description of clumsy incompetence:

tha frames wahr ner a cat i' pattens

Somebody thought by the speaker to be of little moral worth might be described as **nowt a pund** (nothing a pound). Somebody thought to be awkward might be told:

tha's marrer ter Bonny!

This curious expression seems to have originally been 'as marrow to bone' (intimately connected) but in this form dates from the first decades of the nineteenth century, when it could be said that people were **marrers** (exactly like) **Bonny**, that is, Napoleon Bonaparte, who was a byword for ambition and aggression. This WR phrase is matched by a similar usage in NER:

tha 'll nivver see t' marrer tiv 'im
you 'll never see his like

A simple proverb which has not in the least dated, and which I find myself using again and again, is the wise Yorkshire saying:

ther's nowt good that's cheap

And there is the warning not to be deceived by appearances, in a metaphor best understood by **Shevvilders:**

nivver judge a blade bi t' heft (handle)

A personal example of a how a Yorkshire saying can sum up a situation is the comment of an old farmer, quoted when one of our school friends died – the first in our age group:

Aye, lad. The'r takkin 'em aht of ahr pen nah

Best of all is the observation that most of our problems come, not from things, but from the unpredictable behaviour of other people:

ther's nowt so queer as fowk (or **fooaks**)

Finally there is the light-hearted WR extension of this:

**fowks is queer. The'r all queer bar thee an' me –
an' sometimes Ah'm nut so sewer abaht thee!**

Yorkshire similes and insults

Standardised comparisons are very common in Yorkshire dialect. Some of the most vivid are as follows (For vocabulary consult the Yorkshire Dictionary, pages 131-42).

as common as muck
as daft as a brush
as gaumless as a gooise
as sackless as a booat-'oss
as simple as a suckin' duck
as black as t' fire-back
as dark as black coo-skin
as grey as a mowdiwarp
as deeaf as a yat-stowp
as wick as a weasle, kittlin, lop etc.
as waak as a kittlin
as fat as a mawk
as thin as a lat
as straight as a yard o' pump watter
as bald as a blether o' lard
as fahl as a ripped clog
as 'ard as a grundid tooad

as cheerful as chapil-lowsing
as mawngy as an owd cat
as snod as glass
as tough as wengby
as wisht as a mahse
as kittle as a moostthrap
as fierce as a ratten
as slaape as an eel
as drunk as a fuzzock
as druffen as a wheel-'eead
as blinnd as a buzzard
as deep as a draw-well
as crewkt/creeaked as a dog's hind leg
as brant as a 'oose-sahde
as leet as a cleg
as leet-gi'en as a posser-'eead

Three curiosities, whose origins are lost in obscurity, are based on actual people, the first from the Barnsley area:

as idle as Ludlam's dog ('at laid itsen dahn ter bark or 'at leaned it' 'eead agen t' wall ter bark)

as throng as Throp's wife ('oo brewed, weshed an baked on t' same day, then 'enged ersen wi t' dish claht)

as queer as Dick's 'at-band ('at went nine times rahnd, an' wouldn't tee)

In addition, there are various metaphors used as insults: **blether-'eead** (bladder-head), **claht-'eead** (cloth-head), **fond-'eead** (foolish head), **gawp-'eead, lump-yed, daft 'awporth, gommeril** etc, and terms for niggardly people such as **nip-screw** and **nip-curn** (cf 'pinch-penny') and descriptions of a greedy, grasping person:

> **'e's that mean 'e'd nip a curn i' two** WR
> **'e'd skin a lop** (flea) **for t' hide an' t' tallow** NER

Sayings concerning places

Yorkshire humour can sometimes be seen in leg-pulling comments about towns and villages with a reputation they scarcely deserve. An obvious exception is the old prayer 'From Hell, Hull and Halifax good Lord deliver us!', this probably being a reference to the press-gangs in Hull and the guillotine-style 'gibbet' in Halifax.

Some are simply factual, such as the reference to the gypsy horse-fair held in June at Boroughbridge, called Barnaby Fair: 'Barnaby Bright, longest day and shortest night'. Another saying concerning Boroughbridge refers to the Devil's legendary attempt to destroy Aldborough by throwing the monoliths (near Roecliffe) known as the Devil's Arrows:

> **Boroughbrigg keep oot o' t' way,**
> **For Auldboro toon**
> **I'll ding doon**

The women of Bedale, further north, are complimented:

> **Bedale bonnets and Bedale faces**
> **Finnd nowt ti beat 'em**
> **In onny places**

So are the girls of Castleford in the south of the county:

> **Castleford lasses may weel bi fair,**
> **For they wesh i' t' Calder an' sind i' t' Aire**

Halifax, perhaps to compensate for its gibbet, claimed to have similarly attractive girls:

**Halifax is built o' wax
Heptonstall o' stooane;
I' Halifax ther's bonny lasses
I' Heptonstall ther's nooan**

From the Yorkshire coast we have, for example, a jibe at the folk of **Steeas** (Staithes) who picked **flithers** (limpets):

Steeas yackers, flither-pickers, herrin' guts fer garters

The people of Staithes, however, claimed superiority to Runswick, just to the south:

**Runs'ick men wiv all the'r toil
Comes ti Steeas ti sell the'r oil**

To which the folk of Runswick replied:

**Steeas men wiv all the'r nuts
Gans ti Runs'ick ti fill the'r guts**

Knaresborough and Harrogate are referred to in so-called prophecies of Mother Shipton written in dialect after the event:

**When lords an' ladies stinkin' water soss,
High brigs o' steean the Nidd sal cross,
An' a toon be built on Harrogate moss**

When the Knaresborough viaduct collapsed in 1848 the rumour went round the town that Mother Shipton **'allus said 'at big brig across t' Nidd should tummle doon twice an' stand fer ivver when built a third time.'**

Some topographical references have become nicknames: there are, for example, **Leeds Loiners** (from the word for 'lane', thought to be Marsh Lane), **Keighley kay-legged-uns, Wibsa** (Wibsey) and **Pudsa** (Pudsey) **gawbies** (fools), these two places, amongst others, having been described as

wheeare t' ducks fly back'ards ter keep t' muck aht o' the'r een

Various items are associated with particular places, and in dialect literature we may come across Ripon rowels (spurs for which this little city was once famous), the Ripon wakeman or hornblower, a Scarborough warning (a punch first, then the warning), Whitby jet, Staithes bonnets, Dent and its knitters, York chocolate, Pontefract (Pomfret) liquorice, Doncaster butterscotch, Harrogate mineral wells, Denby Dale with its gigantic pie, Sheffield with its world-famous steel, and so forth.

Examples of light-hearted criticisms of Yorkshire places are the following, starting with Great Ayton (where Captain Cook went to school), whose inhabitants are 'Yattoners':

> **Yattoners wade ower t' beck ti seeave** (save) **t' brig**
> **Slowit** (Slaithwaite) **wheeare the' raked mooin aht o' t' cut** (canal)
> **Pontefract – as sewer as a louse i' Pomfret**
> **Ossett, wheeare the' black-leead t' tram-lines**
> **Marsden, wheeare the' put t' pigs on t' wall ter listen ter t' band**
> **Pudsa, wheeare the've all bald 'eeads, cos the' pull 'em aht o' t' pit wi suckers**

A rare example of a compliment used to be found in the advice:

> **Cahr quiet – like the' do i' Birstall**

Yorkshire traditions linked with dialect

Each January in North Yorkshire, especially in Goathland, where the custom was revived by F W Dowson, there is Plough Monday, when lively characters called **pleeaf stots** (literally 'plough bullocks') drag around their plough and perform sword dances.

Before Lent it was customary to use up rich food on **Collop Munda**, with a meal of eggs and **collops** (thick slices) of bacon. The solemn observance of Good Friday in the countryside was reflected in the saying:

On Good Friday rist thy pleeaf;
Start nowt, end nowt: that's eneeaf

Easter is celebrated with **pace-egging** and traditional **pace-egg plays** in the Calder Valley. (**pace** is from Hebrew *pesach*: Passover, Easter.)

All over the county there are ancient fairs, sometimes locally known as **feasts** or **tides**: Ripon's Wilfra Feast (St Wilfrid), Barnsla Feast, Lee Fair, Wibsey Fair, Bowling Tide and Hull Fair, the biggest in Britain. Of particular interest is the custom in the village of West Witton, Wensleydale, of 'Burning Bartle'. On a Saturday near St Bartholomew's Day (24th August) an effigy is burnt after being paraded round the village to the accompaniment of the dialect verse:

At Pen Hill crags he tore his rags,
At Hunter's Thorn he blew his horn,
At Capplebank stee he brak his knee,
At Grassgill Beck he brak his neck,
At Waddam's End he couldn't fend,
At Grassgill End we'll mak his end.
Shout, lads, shout!

In North and East Yorkshire especially there are still memories of ancient harvest rituals, including the **mell-supper** and the cry **We've getten t' mell!** when the harvest was 'safely gathered in'. At harvest festivals and during long sermons at other services, children might be kept quiet by being given **pew spice** (WR) or **goodies** (ER). Coats were hung on prominent pegs, giving rise to the saying that astonished eyes **stuck aht like chapil 'at-pegs.**

One of the most colourful of our folk traditions, November the Fifth, is celebrated with particular enthusiasm in parts of the West Riding, where it is heralded by **Mischief Night** (4th November), and known as **Plot Neet**. It is traditionally prepared for by the collecting of wood, known as **chumpin** or **proggin.**

In the nineteenth century the lads went round begging wood, money and coal, and in the Wilsden area, near Bingley, they would shout a rhyme demanding **'a stick or a stake . . . an 'awpenny or a penny, or else a black coil'**, concluding with the threat **'or else we'll blaw yo' aht o' t' 'oil!'** A similar verse threatened that if the lads were not given **'coil . . . or some sleck'** (slack), they would all come and **'knock off yer dooar sneck'**. The burning of the guy is still accompanied not only by fireworks (once lit by smouldering **mill-band**) but by the distribution of **plot toffee** and **parkin pigs.**

Yorkshire has many folk tales associated with the long winter nights, some concerning **barguests** or evil spirits in the form of a dog, pig, cow etc. Such an apparition could be a portent of death, especially if it was a **guytresh**, with eyes as big as saucers.

Christmas, sometimes written **Kersmass** or **Kessamas** in Yorkshire dialect, used to have all kinds of customs, such as that of **vessil cups**, a box containing a doll (representing the Christ-child in the manger) carried round by children, and singing by **waits** (originally watchmen) and **wassailers**. Carol singing is still known in Yorkshire by the old name of **Christmas singing**.

It is no longer the custom, however, to wish families:

> **A pooakful o' money an' a cellar full o' beer,**
> **A good fat pig an' a new cauven coo**

As well as the burning of yule-logs and the roasting of turkeys (first landed near Bridlington and reared in Boynton in the sixteenth century), two Christmas customs with dialect terms are the eating of **frumenty** or **frumety**, a kind of thick porridge made from hulled wheat, seasoned with sugar and spices such as cinnamon. (When made with barley this dish was known as **fluffin.**) **Spice-cake** is the dialect term for Christmas cake, traditionally accompanied by cheese, especially from Wensleydale.

Yorkshire labels

A Yorkshire Tyke – originally a dog, probably derived from Old Norse *tik* (bitch). It could refer to a snarling, ill-tempered cur, though in some parts of Yorkshire it was an old horse. From the seventeenth century this uncomplimentary name was being applied to wide-awake Yorkshiremen, particularly those from the West Riding. (see p 65)

A Yorkshire bite – a disparaging term applied to Yorkshire dealers, reputed to be sharp and cunning.

A Yorkshireman – a term for a fly found floating on the top of ale; linked with the reputation for cadging a drink.

Yorkshire Terrier – small, long-haired vigorous breed of dog.

Yorkshire Pudding – the batter-pudding that has become Yorkshire's best-known culinary speciality. (see pages 97-98)

Yorkshire Relish – traditional spicy, fruity sauce, made commercially by Goodall and Backhouse (Leeds) from 1837, now by Hammonds. A decision in the House of Lords in 1897 made 'Yorkshire Relish' the only 'geographical trade-mark' of its kind.

Yorkshire Ham – the original term for what is known as 'York ham'.

Yorkshire Mixture – boiled sweets of various shapes and colours.

Yorkshire speyks – sayings or tales in Yorkshire dialect.

Yorkshire Fog – a kind of grass (*holcus lanatus*) found in poor pastures. Fog is also the term for the first grass which grows after mowing.

Yorkshire Rose – a white rose (*rosa alba*) said to have been plucked as his emblem by Richard Plantagenet, Duke of York, at the start of the Wars of the Roses, but already associated with the House of York. It is also the emblem of the King's Own Yorkshire Light Infantry.

Yorkshire Post – newspaper founded in Leeds in 1754.

Yorkshire Dialect Society – founded in Leeds in 1897.

Yorkshire Day – 1st August (day of Battle of Minden 1759), started in 1975 by the Yorkshire Ridings Society, founded the same year.

Yorkshire Society – founded in 1980 to secure 'a better deal for Yorkshire', awards the annual Yorkshire History Prize. Yorkshire societies exist in various towns outside the county, including Birmingham, Edinburgh and London, the latter dating from 1812, and separate from the Society of Yorkshiremen in London, founded in 1899.

Yorkshire – 'a former county in England'! (Concise Oxford Dictionary).

Traditional Yorkshire songs

Let us take as examples two contrasting anonymous songs, the first a dirge which contains pre-Christian elements and was already old when it first appeared in print in 1686. It was sung at funerals in Cleveland, North Yorkshire, and is associated with the Lyke Wake, now well-known through the walk started by Bill Cowley in 1955. The theme is the carrying of the **lyke** (corpse) and the progress of the **sowl** (soul) towards Purgatory and Hell, where good works done in life help to minimise the suffering. This version is the one recorded by Richard Blakeborough:

The Lyke Wake Dirge

This yah neet, this yah neet,
  Ivvery neet an' awl,
Fire an' fleet an' cann'l leet,
  An' Christ tak up thi sowl.

When thoo fra hither gans awaay,
  Ivvery neet an' awl,
Ti Whinny Moor thoo cum'st at last,
  An' Christ tak up thi sowl

If ivver thoo gav' owther hosen or shoon,
  Ivvery neet an' awl,
Clap tha doon an' put 'em on,
  An' Christ tak up thi sowl.

Bud if hosen or shoon thoo nivver ga' neean,
  Ivvery neet an' awl
T' whinnies s'll prick tha sair ti t' beean,
  An' Christ tak up thi sowl.

Fra Whinny Moor that thoo mayst pass,
  Ivvery neet an' awl,
Ti t' Brigg o' Dreead thoo'll cum at last,
  An' Christ tak up thi sowl.

Bud if o' siller an' gawd thoo nivver ga' neean,
  Ivvery neet an' awl,
Thoo'll doon, doon tumm'l tiwards Hell fleeams,
  An' Christ tak up thi sowl.

Fra t' Brigg o' Dreead 'at thoo mayst pass,
  Ivvery neet an' awl,
Ti t' fleeams o' Hell thoo'll cum at last,
  An' Christ tak up thi sowl.

If ivver thoo gav' owther bite or sup,
  Ivvery neet an' awl,
T' fleeams's'll nivver catch tha up,
  An' Christ tak up thi sowl.

But if bite or sup thoo nivver ga' neean,
  Ivvery neet an' awl,
T' fleeams'll bo'n tha sair ti t' beean,
  An' Christ tak up thi sowl.

By way of contrast here is the comparatively recent comic
song that has become a kind of Yorkshire national anthem –
On Ilkla Mooar baht 'at. The words go well with the rousing
Methodist hymn tune 'Cranbrook', composed in 1805 by
Thomas Clark. This, and the words themselves, confirm the
story that this was a leg-pulling bit of verse composed during
or following a choir outing from Halifax in 1886, when the
members walked over Ilkley Moor – no doubt along the well-
worn path from Dick Hudsons – and one of their number went

off with the celebrated Mary Jane to do a bit of courting. He was not wearing a hat – something rather unusual in those days, especially on the breezy moors.

Well-known though the song is, it is often sung very badly, even by Yorkshire people, with the original West Riding dialect giving way to standard English vowels and vocabulary – Ilkley being pronounced 'Ilkli' or 'Ilklay' instead of **Ilkla**, 'more' instead of **mooar**, 'et' instead of **'at**, 'death of cold' instead of **'deeath o' cowd'** etc.

NB Variations on the following are sometimes heard, especially the first line as '*Wheeare es-ta been sin Ah saw thee?*' – but this is a less logical opening, because the courting obviously took place on Ilkley Moor.

On Ilkla Mooar baht 'at

Wheeare wor ta bahn when Ah saw thee
On Ilkla Mooar baht 'at?

Tha's been a-cooartin' Mary Jane . . .

Tha's bahn ter ketch thi deeath o' cowd . . .

Then we s'll 'e ter bury thee . . .

Then t'wurrums 'll come an' eyt thee up . . .

Then t'ducks 'll come an' eyt up t'wurrums . . .

Then we s'll come an' eyt up t'ducks . . .

Then we s'll all 'ev etten thee . . .

That's wheeare wi get us ooan back,

On Ilkla Mooar baht 'at.

Yorkshire Dialect Prose

Whereas dialect verse goes back at least to the *Lyke Wake Dirge* and the period of oral tradition, the recording of dialect speech and the writing of tales in dialect dates principally from the Victorian era.

One of the earliest to make use of local dialect in her writing was Emily Brontë in *Wuthering Heights* (1847). Though there are snatches of Yorkshire dialect in other Brontë novels, notably in Charlotte's *Shirley*, it was Emily Brontë who made a masterly and largely accurate use of the dialect of Haworth, as has been shown by K M Petyt (see Bibliography). Most of the dialect is spoken by the old servant, Joseph, the 'vinegar-faced hypocrite'. Based on a real person, he is an extreme Calvinist who prides himself that he is one of 'them as is chozzen', and picked out from the rubbish of unsaved sinners. In the first edition of 1847 we can see how carefully Emily has tried to convey the sounds of the dialect she heard all round her in Haworth. In later editions, however, her spelling of words like **dahn** and **nooin** was modified to 'down' and 'noon' by Charlotte, who made various other changes to make the dialect easier to read. The following extracts are from the original edition.

Joseph in *Wuthering Heights* (extracts)

'T' maisters dahn i' t' fowld. Goa rahnd by th'end ut' laith, if yah went tuh spake tull him.'

'They's nobbut t' missis; and shoo'll nut oppen 't, an (if) ye mak yer flaysome dins till neeght.'

'Aw woonder hagh yah can faishion tuh stand thear i' idleness un war, when all on 'em's goan aght! Bud yah're a nowt, and it's noa use talking – yah'll niver mend uh yer ill ways; bud, goa raight tuh t' divil, like yer mother afore ye!'

'T' maister nobbut just buried, and Sabbath nut oe'red, and t' sahnd uh t' gospel still i' yer lugs, and yah darr be laiking!

shame on ye! sit ye dahn, ill childer! they's good books eneugh
if ye'll read 'em; sit ye dahn and think uh yer sowls!

'Maister Hindley!' . . . 'Maister, coom hither! Miss Cathy's
riven th' back off 'Th' Helmet uh Salvation', un' Heathcliff's
pawsed his fit intuh t' first part uh 'T' Brooad Way to
Destruction!' It's fair flaysome ut yah let 'em goa on this gait.
Ech! th'owd man ud uh laced 'em properly – bud he's goan!'

'Yon lad gets war un war!' . . . 'He's left th' yate ut t' full
swing, and miss's pony has trodden dahn two rigs uh corn, un
plottered through, raight o'er intuh t' meadow! Hahsomdiver,
t' maister 'ull play t' divil to-morn, and he'll do weel.

'Aw sud more likker look for th' horse' . . . 'It 'ud be tuh
more sense. Bud, aw can look for norther horse, nur man uf a
neeght loike this – as black as t' chimbley! und Hathecliff's
noan t'chap tuh coom ut maw whistle – happen he'll be less
hard uh hearing wi ye!'

'Nay, nay, he's noan at Gimmerton!' . . . 'Aw's niver
wonder, bud he's at t' bothom uf a bog-hoile. This visitation
worn't for nowt, und aw wod hev ye tuh look aht, Miss, yah
mud be t'next. Thank Hivin for all! All warks togither for gooid
tuh them as is chozzen, and picked aht froo th' rubbidge! Tah
knaw whet t' Scripture ses –'

'Running after t' lads, as usuald!' . . . 'It's bonny behaviour,
lurking amangt' fields after twelve ut' night, wi that fahl,
flaysome divil uf a gipsy, Heathcliffe! Theyd think Aw'm blind;
but Aw'm noan, nowt ut t' soart! Aw seed young Linton, boath
coming and going, and Aw seed yah' . . . 'Yah gooid fur nowt,
slattenly witch! nip up und bolt intuh th' hahs, t' minute yah
heard t' maister's horse fit clatter up t' road!'

From the East Riding here is a typical folk-tale of unknown
date. This is based on the version written down by M F C
Morris in 1892.

T' Moos i' t' vat

Ther wer yance a moos 'at had gitten it hooal just agaan a

greeat vat iv a briewery. T' vat were full o' liquor iv a gen'ral waay, an' yah day t' lahtle moos chanced ti tumm'l in, an' were leyke ti be dhroonded.

'An' seea', says t' moos tiv itsen, 'What mun Ah deea? T' sahds is seea slaap an' brant Ah doot Ah sa'll nivver git yam na mair; Ah's flaayed Ah sa'll 'a' ti gan roond an' roond whahl Ah's dhroonded.'

Bud eftther a bit t' cat pops it heead ower t' top o't' vat, an' sha leeaks at t' moos an' says, 'What wilt tha gie ma if Ah git tha oot o't' vat?' 'Whya,' says t' moos, 'thoo s'all 'a' ma'.

'Varry weel,' says t'cat, an' seea sha hings hersen doon o' t'insahd; t' moos varry seean ran up t' cat back and lowp'd reet fra t' top o' t' vat intiv it hooal, an' t' cat eftther it.

Bud t' moos were ower sharp an' gat fo'st ti t' hooal, an' then to'ns roond an starts ti laff at t' cat. T' cat wer ommost wahld at that, an' shoots oot, 'Didn't thoo saay 'at if Ah gat tha oot o' t' vat Ah sud 'a' tha?' 'Aw,' says t' moos, 'Aw', shoo says, 'Bud fowks 'll saay owt when the're i dhrink!'

From Emily Brontë's Joseph onwards, Yorkshire dialect prose has always been essentially humorous. William Cudworth of Bradford collected material at the end of the nineteenth century, including such tales as the following from his *Yorkshire Speyks*. Actual places are referred to – Wibsey, Bankfoot, Bowling Lane, Manor Row etc – and actual people, such as Joe Wreet, the well-known Wibsey headmaster, Joseph Wright.

Dicky Dunnaker's search for a Wife

Ye wodden't think it, happen, but Dicky Dunnaker belenged t' aristockracy o' Wibsa'. His fatther, Doady, hed thriven o' coil-leadin' an' deealin' i' spavvined 'osses, an' med brass eniff ta retire. Althaw he lived in his awn hahse, an' wor called gentleman' i' t' votin' lists, Dicky's fatther heddent mich ov a lewk o' one, as he wor nivver seen baht smock an' knee-britches, same as he ware when he wor coil-leadin'. . .

Nah Dicky wor raythur a different sooart ov a chap tuv his fatther, for he'd been to Joe Wreet schooil, an' they allus said if it wor possible to drive larnin' thru a deel booard, Joe Wreet cud dut. Ah doan't think he manidged soa weel wi' Dicky Dunnaker. For sewer, he cud write his naame, after a feshun, an' reckoned to be a dab hand at figgers; bud onny Booard-schooiler nah-a-days wod 'a licked him inta fits.

Dicky hed getten to be a man o' thirty when his fatther deed, bud he wor nivver fond o' wark. He'd hallack his time away cummin' thru t' pit whol gettin' intut afternooin, an' he'd 'a gooan tappin' at t' dooars i' Bowlin' Loin an' sayin': 'Nah, missis, can ye dew wi' a looad o' nice coils? T' fowk 'at Ah browt 'em for hes flitten, an' Ah'd loise bi' em raythur nor tak' 'em hooam.'

This wor abaht as big a bit o' lyin' as Dicky wor capable on; an' as for givin' short weight, wah, ov course, that worrent lewked on as a sin i' them days, becos all coil-leaders did it.

Bud when owd Doady deed an' left him his brass, Dicky didn't want onny excuse to drop coil-leadin'. As he said, he'd plenty ta live on, so what wor t' use ov killin' issen wi' warkin'?

Ah hardly need say 'at Dicky hed nivver getten wed. Boath him an' his fatther hed scraaped along withaht wommanly help, except nah an' then, when Susy o'Nans, or Tahn-end Betty, wor called in to wesh ther' things as neer white as they'd cum. . ..

At onnyrate, Dicky wor nah left to shift for hissen, an' a bonny shift he made on't. He wor t'warst put tult wi' t' bakin'. One day he thowt he'd try his hand at a potaty pie, bud when he'd getten t'crust on, t' ovven wor soa cowd whol t'taties tuk rooit an' grew aht o' t'top befoar it wor reddy. Soa they us't to say at Benkfooit, but Ah think they must ha' ratched it a bit. As for blackleeadin', or ironin' his shirts, Dicky fairly duffed, till boath t'hahse an' hissen wor ashaamed to be seen.

'Begow, Dicky,' he sed tuv hissen one mornin' i' bed, 'this an' better may dew, but this an' wahr, nivver. Tha mun hev a wife, cost what it may.'. . . .

He'd heeard tell o' gettin' wed at t' Regester Office, soa he judged 'at they fun 'em wives as weel. Soa up he jumped, donned hissen as smart as ninepence, an' set off to Bradford. He'd been i' sich a hurry whol it worn't aboon hawf-passt eight when he rapt at t'Regester Office doar i' Manner Raw. It wor too sooin for t' regester man – for them chaps doan't begin a-lakin' whol abaht ten o'clock. After a bit he rapped ageean, an' a chap cam' tu't doar wi' a brush in his hand.

'Ah say, mate,' sez Dicky, 'isn't this t' Regester Office?'

'Aye, for sewer it is,' sez t' chap wi' t' brush, 'bud yer too sooin. Hev ye browt t' young woman?'

'Noa!' sez Dicky, 'becos Ah hevn't one. Ah thowt happen ye kept a few i' stock here.'

Weel ye'st 'a seen t' chap wi' t' brush, hah he ommost brust wi' laffin'. Bud he bethowt him he wodn't, cos he ment to hev a bit mooar fun aht o' Dicky. So he sez:

'Wah, ye see t'regester isn't cum yet or else he'd knaw. Happen ye can wait a bit?'

'Haugh, for sewer,' sez Dicky. 'Ah'm nooan perticler tuv an hahr or two.'

It wor a cowd mornin', an' ther' wor no fire i' t' hoil, so when Dicky hed gaped whol he wor ommost frozzen to deeath, he began stampin' abaht t' flooer. Presently a yung swell cam' an' went intuv a room wi' a glass winda 'at slid up an' dahn, marked 'Inquire here,' an' t' chap wi' t' brush followed him in. Dicky heeard 'em laffin' an' tawkin' inside, bud he thowt nowt abaht that. Presently t' glass winda slotted up an' t'yung swell sez: 'What's your business, sir?'

'If this is t' Regester Office,' says Dicky, 'da ye think ye can finnd ma a yung wumman 'at 'll mak' ma a deeacent wife? Ah'm happen nut mich to lewk at, bud Ah'm nooan baht brass.'

Weel, it tewk all t' swell's pahrs to keep thru laffin' reyt aht, bud he sed he'd see, an' dahn went t' winda. In a bit he heeard 'em tawkin' an' laffin' inside, an' first one an' then another

cam' to hev a lewk at him. In a bit t' first chap cum an' sed
'at they thowt they cud fit him up, bud he'd hetta cum ageean
an' bring sumboddy to give him away.' Dicky wor raythur capt
wi' that, bud as he'd heeard summat abaht givin' away at
weddin's he thowt it wor all reyt.

Wi' this Dicky went hooam like a lark, and telled t' nayburs
hah he'd cum on. By dewin' soa he spoiled t' gam', for asteead
o' carryin' on't on they telled him what a fooil they wor bahn
to mak' on him, an' Dicky believed it soa whol he nivver went
tu t' Regester Office ageean.

A brilliant observer of Yorkshire life and speech was the Rev
Walter F Turner, whose *Goodies* was first published in 1912
(reprinted by the YDS in 1990). The first of his stories is
typical of those which are still popular when read by a dialect
speaker in public. This, like all Walter Turner's stories, is in
East Riding dialect and his quaint spelling has been retained.

Goodies

It fair caps me what for fooaks want te it goodies i' Choch!
Yan wad reallye think 'at soomm fooaks couldn't saah ther
prayers wivoot a goody i' ther moothes. It caps owt! It dis, Ah
seer.

T' parson o' Soondah ad nobbut joost getten inti t' pew, an
a fat oard woman i' t' seeat i' froont o' me thowt sher were
fooast te ev a goody. An sher parzels 'er and awaah roond tiv'
er greeat oard pockit at t' back, an' began scrattin aboot, an
rattlin kays an paaper an sike like, te see if sher could finnd a
bit o' goody. An there sher war laatin an scrattin aboot, like a
'en on a moock middin, wharl wer gat te t' Psalms.

An sher gat that vexed, becos sher couldn't finnd yan
o'onny, sher could scaarce bard. Sher bleeamed t' bairns, yer
knaw, for gerrin tiv 'er pockit throoff t' week. Sher knawed
sher'd left twe or tree o't' lasst Soondah, d'yer see? or else sher
wad a gettin soomm mare when sher were i' Pickering Set'dah

neet; bud noo sher couldn't finnd yan, naather a mint, ner a rooase, ner a acid, ner a anise, ner owt.

Awivver sher were despert jealous sher owt te ev a goody iv er pockit soomwheres, d'yer see? Seea i' t' fosst Lesson sher'd ev anoother laat. An sher began to tak t'things oot of er pockit this tahme, d'yer see? an put em doon i' t' seeat ageean er.

By Lad! Ah wadn't like to be a woman an nobbut a yar pockit, an that awaah roond at t' back, where ye' etti crick yer neck an put yer shooder oot te ger at it. Ah wadn't awivver!

Ah tell yer what, lads, if you ad seen what a greeat vasst o' things that there woman ad i' yar pockit; an t' tewin, an t' scrattin, an t' twistin sher ad te ger a bit o' goody oot at warn't there, yer'd sympathahse wiv em, Ah tell yer, when ther want te ger inti, what ther call, rational costume.

Look yer! Ah couldn't fairly tell yer what there wasn't i' that there woman pockit! Ah joost shoott me eese, an oppened em ageean, an Ah thowt Ah were at a joomle saale i'steead o' i' t' Choch, Ah did awivver! Ah ev thotteen pockits mesen, an, look yer, Ah ayant as monny things i' all on em tegither as what that there woman ad i' urr yan, Ah seer Ah ayant.

There was t'doer kay, there was a anketcher, there was a bootten ook, there was a kettle odder, there was fower or fahve bits o' band, there was a thimmle, there was a pincushin, there was a posse, there was a yed measure, there was aaf a doozzen airpins lapped oopp iv a bit o' paaper – Ah knaw ther were airpins, becos sher oppened em oot, sher thowt t' goody ad mebbe getten amang em, d'yer see? an there was soommat else, Ah've forgetten what. Ohr eye, there was a bit o' pencil wi' t' point brokken, an there was a cleease pin, an a bit o' wax, an despert thrang deed o' boottons, an bits o' paaper at ad mebbe ad goodies in em at soomm tahme, an a deal mare things.

An ther were all i' yar pockit! That's what capped me. Oo-an-ivver sher gat em in Ah deean't knaw. An Ah were matched te knaw oo sher were gahin te ger em in ageean afoor t' Choch loused, bud awivver sher did.

An sher went reet awaah doon inti t' boddom o' that there

pockit, an sher rowed aboot, an laated i' t' coorners, an sher couldn't finnd a bit o' goody deeah what sher wad, there warn't yan.

By Lad! she did luke vexed!

An sher began te sooart o' sooart t' things ower, an trust em back intiv er pockit ageean. An sher put t' doer kay in at t' boddom, yer knaw. becos it us be t' fosst thing sher'd want oot; – an then sher put er anketcher in, an then t' rist o' t' things. Awivver sher gat em all rammled in a deal sharper an Ah could o' reckoned on.

An then sher leeaned back i' t' seeat te ev a rist, an Ah's think sher wanted yan, sher were varry near tewed te deeath. An Ah thowt sher'd deean wiv er oard pockit for yar sarvice awivver.

Bud joost as t' parson began is sarmon an ad gin oot t' text, t'woman wanted er anketcher, an sher ad te gan tiv er pockit ageean. An sher gat odden t' anketcher be t' coorner an raave it oot. An t' thimmle com oot wiv it, d'yer see? an t' thimmle rattled doon onti t' seeat, d'yer see? An, by Lad! there was a goody toommled oot o' t' thimmle!

Ah nivver seed neeabody se pleased i' me wick! Sher were fair capped, was t' woman. An sher popped t' goody intiv er mooth, an by Goom! it were a mint! an a despert strang un an all, it fair reeked all ower t' Choch! An there sher set knappin an knappin awaah like a steeanchecker. An then sher stack a bit on't awaa inti t' coorner of er cheek, te mak it lasst, an listened te t' sarmon mebbe a minute, or mebbe twea. An then sher started scroonchin awaa ageean, like an oard ratten at t' back of a skettin booard, wharl sher'd getten it deean.

An then sher tooke t'thimmle oot ageean, te see if there were onny mare goodies getten in, but there warn't.

An afoor Ah knawed where Ah war, t' sarmon was owerd wiv, an all Ah'd eeard on't was t', text, 'Tak neeah thowt for the morrer.' An seeah wer coommed awaa oot. An Ah knaw t'oard woman were thinkin all t' tahme sher'd etti ev soomm mare goodies getten afoor t' next Soondah.

Ohr, them goodies! Ah deean't knaw what maks fooaks se craazed on em, Ah deean't Ah seer. Noo Ah can chow mah bit o' bacca i' t' Choch an nivver mak a soond wiv it, an nivver neeabody knaw nowt at all aboot it.

The West Riding almanacks provide us with a wealth of information about the life of working folk in the industrial towns of Yorkshire - the dominance of the mill and mine, the simplicity of domestic life, home-made entertainment and humour. Here is an example of almanack humour from one of the later issues of *The Colne Valley Almanack* (1932), a satire on one of the great cultural contributions of the West Riding, the Huddersfield Choral Society, famed for its performances of Handel's *Messiah:*

Goin' to t' Messiah

Two Golcar chaps were walking down Scar Lane one cold December day, when one said:

'Ah'm thinkin' o' goin' to t' Messiah i' th' Huddersfild Taan Hall next Friday neet. Will ta go wi mi, Bill?'

'Nay, music's nowt i' my line. Ah like a gooid comic song or a lively jig, but Ah mek nowt o' this sacred stuff, as they call it. It's a bit aboon me. An' Ah reckon there'll be nooan o' yar sooart there; mostly religious folk and swells donned i' boiled shirts, an' women wi' nowt mich on. Now, tha mun goa bi thiseln, and tell me all abaat it some time.

During the following week these pals met again, when the following conversation took place:

'Oh, it wor fair champion, lad. Ah wodn't ha missed it for a dollar. When Ah gate theear t' Taan Hall were craaded, choc full o' folk; t' organ chap were laakin' abaat like wi t' organ, playing nowt perticlar, nobbut running his fingers up an' daan as if he wor practisin', like yar Martha used to do when shoo

started learnin' ta play t' piano. Then they brought t' Messiah
in – at ony rate what Ah took ta be it. It wor t' biggest
instrument on t' platform, an' it wor covered wi' a green bag.
When they'd takken it aat o' t' bag, a chap rubbed it belly wi'
a stick, an' tha sud ha' yerd it groaan. It wor summat like t'
last expirin' mooan of a dying caa. It worn't mich better when
he started t' twitchin' it yeroil up, an' in a bit a chap came on
donned in a white waistcoit an' everything wor as quiet as a
maase.

'He 'ad a stick, an' he used it an' all to some tune, Ah'll tell
thi. If tha asks me, he ought ta ha' walloped some o' them
chaps 'at wor reckonin' ta sing. They hadn't been goin' long
afore they wor fratchin' like cats. One side said they wor t'
King o' glory, and' t' other side said they wor, so which side
really won Ah've no idea. Ah think they ought to ha' gooan to
Leeds Road next day and settled it theer.

'Then there wor a bit o' bother abaat some sheep 'at wor
lost. Ah don't know who they belonged to, but they must ha'
been champion twisters and turners judgin' bi t' words an
fancy music. One lot o' singers must ha been very fond o'
mutton, because they kept on saying "All we like sheep." Ah
couldn't help saying to a chap sat next to me "It's all reight is
sheep i' moderation, but gi me a bit o' beef underdone." He
looked daggers at me and said "Shush". So Ah shushed.

'In a bit a big chap gaat on his feet an' started singin. Ah
wish tha could ha heeard him. He'd a voice like owd Jabez
Shaw, o' Linfit, who once freetened all t' folk on Blackpool
Promenade when he went to t' top o' t' Tower an started
shaatin' "View, Alloa," just like he did when he wor huntin
on Blackmoorfooit. Well, this chap wor as mad as blazes, an
singin summat abaat t' heathen ragin together, an t' band wor
just as furious, they saiged away at ther fiddles whol Ah'm
certain ther arms warked.

'Ah wor feelin a bit stiff an a bit stalled Ah'm baan to
confess, when everybody i' t' audience stood up, an t' band an
singers an a chap wi a long trumpet, started t' Halleluyah

Chorus. By gum, lad, it wor fair grand. It med mi back go into cold shivers, specially when they said it wor baan to rain for ivver an ivver. Ah'd had mi bob's worth, so Ah pushed mi way aat, an made mi way to t'station afore t' rain came on, as Ah'd forgotten mi umbrella.'

It is interesting to follow this tale with a version of it in East Riding dialect provided by Arthur Jarratt and published in the YDS *Summer Bulletin* (1985):

T' Messiah (Holderness version)

A farmer was given a ticket to a performance of 'Messiah'. He had not heard it, or any other oratorio before, and this is how he described it to a neighbour:

'Well noo t' spot was ommost full, an Ah'd a job ti finnd missen a seeat. Hooiver, Ah did, an then they started ti fill up t' platform wiv a lot o chaps aall dressed up i white shot fronts. They leeaked as thaw they'd aall left their weskits at yam. Hooiver they'd aall gotten a fiddle apeeace, an mah wod, they did leeak grand.

Noo when they were aall sattled doon, they browt in a sooalin greeat creeatur iv a green bag. They took aall his clooas off, then they screwed up his lugholes wahl he fairly creeaked. Then they scraaped a white stick ower his chest, an by lad, thoo niver heeard siken a grooan.

Then a lartle chap cummed in wiv a stick iv his hand, and started ti waave it aall ower spot, and some moore chaps i white dickies thowt he'd gone balmy way they leeaked at him. Sooa they shooted at him aboot some sheeap that ed gotten lost. Ah deeant knaw hoo monny on em there was, or what they were woth, but yan thing was sartin – they'd aall gotten lost.

Then a chap got up an sung by hissen. Ah think they must a bin his sheeap somebody ed tekken, cos he said they imagined a vaan thing. He soonded raavin mad – an t' organist he soonded mad an aall. Ah wor glad when fella sat hissen doon.

Then a lot of women got owerend. They aall lewked as though they wor gettin on a bit. They sang "Unto Us A Child is Born" and t' fellas at t' other end shooted back "Wonderful! Wonderful!" An Ah thowt t' saame. There wasn't yan on em under sixty.

Then a chap stood up an said he was t' King o Kings, and then another said he was – an they started faallin oot. Then when t' audience aall stood up ti see what was t' matther they sang "Halleluyah! It's off ti raain for ivver and ivver!"

Ah thowt bi this Ah'd had plenty, so Ah got mi hat and med for dooer. Ah thowt Ah'd better get yam afoor t' flood caame. It was a good do tho. But Ah do hoaap them sheeap tonned up.'

A picture of daily domestic routine in the early years of the twentieth century is provided by these reminiscences (not strictly autobiograpical) given by Horace Kellett of Wibsey, published in the YDS *Summer Bulletin*, 1975.

Wick in an' Wick aht

By gum! Ah'd summat on when Ah wor a lad! After mi muther deed Ah wor browt up bi two maiden ants. T' younger on 'em wor called Marth' Ann. She wor a weyver, an' she shahted a lot. I' them days weyvers allus seemed to shaht. Ah suppoase it wor wi bawlin ower t' top o' t' loom to ther beam-mate, or across t' alley to ther elbow-mate. T' owdest ant wor called Sar' Ann, an' she stopped at ooame an' did t' ahse work while Ah went to t' schooil. She wor a tarter, an' all. Talk abaht strict! Ivverything 'ad to be done same as if it wor bi an act o' Parlyment . . .

Munda (Wesh Day). There wor allus a bit of a fratch of a

Munda mornin. We'd ter ger aht o' bed an ahr sooiner, an' ger all t' weshin tackle ready afooare ther wor owt t' eyt. It wor my job to leet t' set pot, fill it wi' watter, an' then lig t' thible on t'top so it wornt to seek when Aunt Sar' Ann wanted to stir t' weshin. After this Ah'd ter put t' piggin back under t' sink an bring t' posser an' t' voider aht.

When Ah come 'ooame for mi dinner t' place 'ud bi full o' steam, an' as sooin as Ah oppened t'door Aunt Sar' Ann 'ould shaht aht:

'Nah, doff thi coit lad, an' come an' twind t' wringer.'

It took some twindin did yon mengle. It did that! While Ah struggled away Ant Sar' Ann 'ould shove clooathes through, an' when she'd done slahtin abaht we'd sit dahn to wer dinner. On a Munda it wor allus cowd meyt an' pickled onions. An' Ah remember 'at yon onions ewsed to give Ant Sar' Ann a lot o' wind. She nivver said: 'Excuse me', same as they do today. She just said: 'Drat them there onions! Ah weeant ev ony mooare!' But she allus did.

When Ah come back from schooil at tea-time she'd still be agate wi t' weshing. Ah 'ed to side some o' t' tackle, roll t' carpet back, an' mop t' stooane floor. Then Ah'd dash off to t' paper-shop at t' corner an' liver mi evenin papers. Ah got awf a crahn a week for it – which wor nooan so bad, for a lad o' twelve.

When Ah 'ad mi teea ther seeamed to be weshin all ovver t'shop. Ah couldn't see t' fire for t' gurt big clooathes-'oss, an ther wor clooathes lines across t' 'arth decked wi shirts an pants, an women's stuff, all 'anging dahn from t' breead-fleg.

Tuesda (Ironin Day). Ah'd an 'ahr longer i' bed, an' Ah'd get up abaht awf past seven. Wi lived in a back-ter-back, tha knaws, an t' closit were dahn t' yard. It wor a cowd do i' winter, Ah'll tell thi.

On a Tuesda ther wor allus kippers for teea, an then t' ironin 'ould start. It wor a big job, wi t' table cleared, an a two-a-thri flat-irons on t' go. Ah wor glad to gerr aht an laik wi t' lads, bud when Ah got back at t' supper-time, it wor grand to be able to see t' fire ageean. Bi t' time Ah wor eatin mi tea-cake mooast o' t'clooathes were fowlded up, an' mi two ants 'ould be darnin stockings. Ah'd leet mi cannle an' set off upstairs, an' this time Ant Marth' Ann 'ould appen bawl after me:

'Think on! Mind tha doesn't spill onny cannle-fat on t' flooar!'

Wedn'sda (Shoppin' Day). Ivvery Wedn'sda Ant Sar' Ann went to t' Co-op an bowt all sooarts o' grooaceries – but there wer nowt tasty for dinner. It wor allus fried spuds flavoured wi a bit of o' mahse-trap cheese, what wi called wengby, cos it wor as tough as leather. T' seet on it used to mak me gip, bud Aunt Sar' Ann ewsed to stand ower me an' mak me eyt it up.

Still, there wor summat on a Wedn'sda at seeamed like a real treat – fish an' chips for teea. After Ah'd livered mi papers Ah'd ter go dahn ter t'fish-'oil. I' them days all three on us could get a meal for fowerpence-'awfpenny. Fish wor a penny, chips nobbut a 'awfpenny.

Thursda (Bakin Day). T'best day o' t' week! Ee, Thursdas wor grand i' winter. Plenty o' coil on t' fire to get t' oven 'ot, an' when Ah come 'ooame at dinnertime, what a glorious smell ther wor comin aht o' yond oven! Ant Sar' Ann 'ould be ewsin' t'table-top, chucking t'dooaf abaht, brayin it wi t' rollin pin, clahtin it wi er fist nah an' ageean, then cuttin lumps off to fit into t' looaf tins, which she put into t' fender. While she wor waitin for t' dooaf to rise she'd roll aht t' curn teea-cakes an set abaht makkin fattie-cakes an moggy. Ee, it wor grand wor all yon bakin when it come aht o' t' oven – both t' smell on it an' t' seet on it. By gum! Ivvery Thursda mi gob wattered same as its nivver done sin.

Frida (Fettlin Day). This wor t' wust day o' t' week. Ah 'ed ter ger up an ahr sooiner an' shift all t' chairs an' t' sofa aht o' t' rooad. Bi t'time t' two ants 'ed finished, t' ahse wer rivven i' bits. Ther wor nooa fire, an t' watter 'ed ter be boiled on t' gas-ring. As sooin as Ant Marth' Ann wor off to 'er wark Ant

Sar' Ann 'ould start black-leadin an brasso-in, an' bi t'time
Ah come ooame fer mi dinner sh'd fettled t' brass fender (t'
one 'at they browt aht at week-ends, tha knaws) cleaned all t'
orniments, weshed t' pot dogs on t' mantlepiece, an' polished
t' knob on t' oven dooar till it shone as breet as a full mooin.
Dinner wor allus t' same on Fettlin' Day – cowd meyt pie.

When Ah come oame after mi paper rahnd, Aunt Marth'
Ann ould ave just nicely finished swillin t' flegs an' scahrin t'
dooarst'n. Ah can 'ear 'er nah bawlin at me: 'Tha mun wipe
thi feet afooare tha comes in 'ere! Dooan't thee trail onny muck
into t' ahse or tha'll feel t' back o' my 'and!' Mind you, when
Ah did get inside Ah will admit it allus looked reight cosy.
Ivverythin wor streight, an t' fire wor blazing away all breet
an' friendly in t' gleamin surrahnd. Aye, even as a lad, Ah wor
glad ter see t' ahse fettled.

Setterda (Laikin Day) No schooil on a Setterda, so Ah could
lig i' bed a bit longer, an mooast o' t' day Ah could do owt Ah
wanted – appen laik at taws, or fooitball, or just mullock abaht.
We' ed sausages fer dinner of a Setterda – two apiece – wi
mashed pertaties, an' as sooin as it wor ower, an t' pots wor
weshed, aht 'ould come t' brass fender – an t' owd iron fender
wor sided till Sunda neet. Then they'd put a plush green cover
ower t' table, wi t' aspidestra plonked i' t' middle

Sunda (Chapil Day). Sunda mornin they saw to it at Ah ed
a reight gooid wesh afooare Ah put mi Sunda clooathes on. T'
owd ants ewsed ter don theresens up i ther Sunda best, wi
black skirts nearly touchin t' flooar, an laced-up booits
underneath – but yer nivver saw owt o' t' booits till they sat
thersens dahn. When we set off they'd don ther Sunda 'ats, all
covered i flahrs, an wi gurt big 'at-pins stickin' aht an lookin
as if they went reight through ther 'eeads an' come aht at t'
other side.

Well, they'd go ter t' chapil while Ah went ter t' Sunda
Schooil, an then Ah'd come 'ooame in 'igh spirits ready fer t'
Sunda dinner. It wor a champion meal, even though it wor
allus t' same – rooast beef an' Yorkshire Puddin. After dinner

Ah could read mi comic, an t' ants 'ould read t' Sunda Cumpanion. Ah remember there wor nooa sahnd save t' tickin' o' t' owd gran'fatther clock an' t' rustlin o t' paper. They'd read 'awf on it apiece, tha sees, then swop ower.

Ah'd ter gooa ter t' Sunda Schooil ageean i' t' afternooin, an' they med me go wi em ter t' chapil at neet. Ah dursn't mak onny complaints, bud if ivver Ah looked a bit dahn i' t' mahth abaht it Ant Sar'Ann 'ould say: 'Tha's nooan laikin aht on a Sunda, bud if tha be'aves thissen tha'll appen get some peew-spice.'

Well, at awf past eight Ah ed mi biscuit an' a sup o' milk, an' as Ah med mi way up t' stairs bi t' flickerin leet o' mi cannle, t' maiden ants 'ould start ter side t' green table-cover, swop t' brass fender fer t' iron 'n, an' put t' aspidestra back in t' winder bottom. Last of all they'd wind t' gran'fatther clock up so's it could start another wick's wark, tellin ivvery ahr o t' day, tickin' an' strikin' away ter regerlate wer clock-wark lives - t' same owd thing, wick in, an' wick aht.

Yorkshire pudding is not the easiest dish to make to perfection. Here are some of the trade secrets disclosed by a 'Wawdswoman', a housewife from the Yorkshire Wolds (YDS *Transactions*, 1937):

Yorkshire Pudding

Ere's oo a Waudswoman maks Yorkshire puddin. Allus measure t' flooer, an alloo yah taablespeeanful (nut a big un) ti yah person. Ti ivvery tweea speeanfuls o' flooer alloo yah egg, an yer'll ev a good puddin. But if yer want a varry special un – when comp'ny's comin, like – then alloo yah egg ti yah speeanful o' flooer, an yer'll ev a topper.

Put t' flooer in a baasin, add a bit o' salt, but deean't put in neea bakin pooder. Brek t' eggs intit flooer an beeat wi a wooden speean whahl yet get all lahtle lumps oot. Poower in a sup o' milk, an gan on wi yer beeatin; then a lahtle sup o' caud watther, an beeat ageean. T' puddin'll be sad if yer use

all milk an neea watther: yer want aboot yah part watther ti
three parts milk. Mix t' puddin same as yer mix lithin: it mun
be aboot as thick as creeam.

Let t' puddin stand a bit, fra thotty minutes ti an oor. Then
melt some fat in a drippin-tin, just eneeaf fat ti cover bottom
o' t' tin, an poower t' puddin in. Baake whahl t' puddin rises
ti t' top er t' tin, an is yaller-broon all ower. Yer mun mahnd
ti ev t' oven yat. Puddin ween't rise if t' oven's ower caud.

Cut t' puddin i' squares, an sarve it quick, wi some good
broon graavy, afore yer ev t' meeat.

During the Second World War the Bradford *Telegraph and
Argus* raised morale on Friday nights with the rich dialect
stories 'bi Buxom Betty'. These were all written by Emily
Denby, born and bred at Tong Park, Baildon. She started soon
after the joining the *Telegraph* in 1919 and kept the stories
going for nearly thirty years. There is not space to do justice
to the homely humour of the Higginbottams and Nimble-
tongues, but here is a short extract from her account of 't'
mothers' meetin' at t' chapil':

'The're nutmegs,' said Missis Cappem. It's a reight owd
remedy 'at's been handed dahn i' ahr fambly fer generations.
Mi grandmother did it, an' sooa did mi gurt grandmother.
There's nowt like sewin hawf a dozen nutmegs rahnd yer
garters fer keepin t' rheumatics away'. . .

'Well, ther's this abaht it,' spak up Missis Nimbletongue.
'They say 'at them 'at suffers wi' t' rheumatics isn't bothered
wi' onny other sooarts o' ailments, sooa that's summat to be
thankful for.'

'Is it?' said Missis Twistem. 'Ah sud think t' rheumatics is
bad eniff baht hevin owt else to put up wi'. Ah think sooa,
onnyway, but Ah'll try t' mustard i' mi shooin' an' t' nutmegs
i' mi garters, an' see hah Ah goa on,'

Just then t'owd chapil caretakker come hobblin in, an' Missis Higginbottam handed him a chair an' said: 'Hah's yahr rheumatics goin on, Joany?'

'Haw, nooan so bad, consitherin t' weather,' said Joany, 'but yo' knaw, Ah've getten agate o' huggin a raw tatie i' awther pocket o' mi trahses, an' they say it's a sewer cure, sooa Ah'm hoapin' to be all reight bi t'time t' sun shines an t' cuckoo sings.'

'Aye, we s'll all breeten up when t' weather mends,' said Missis Nimbletongue. 'An' nah, hedn't we better sing a hymn an' lowse t' meetin'. It's ommost fower o'clock. Missis Binns, will yo' strike up t' doxology?'

Kit Calvert MBE of Hawes, famous for his second-hand book-shop and his revival of Wensleydale cheese-making, was a great Dales character and dialect-speaker. He 'translated' several passages of the New Testament into Wensleydale dialect, including this from St Luke's Gospel.

St Luke's Gospel: Chapter Fifteen

Noo, awl t' taxgitherers an' knockaboots crooded roond ta hear Him, an' t' Pharasees an' t' lawyers chuntered an' said, 'This feller tek's up wi' good-fer-nowts an' eyts wi' 'em.'

Sooa, He told 'em this teeale, an' said: 'Whar's t' man amang ye, if he hed a hunderd sheep, an' lost yan on 'em, 'at wadn't leeave awl t' others on t' fell an' gang an' laate t' straggler till he finnds it? An' when he does leet on 't wadn't he lift it ontev his shooders an' hug 't heeame fain an' glad, an' send roond tev his friends an' naybers ta let 'em knaa 'at t' straggler 'd turned up? An' Ah's tellen ye, it's seeame i' heaven. Ther's maar joy ower yah sinner 'at's gitten back, ner ther' is ower ninety-nine 'at yan's nivver had ta laate.

Er what wumman wi' ten bits o' silver, if she was ta loss yan on 'em, wadn't leet a cannel an' ratch ivvery neuk an' coorner

Kit Calvert.

till she finnds it? An' when she hez fun 't, she coa's awl t' naybers tigither an sez, 'Sharr wi' mi i' mi joy, fer Ah've fun mi silver penny 'at Ah'd lost.' It's just seeame amang t'Angils o' God, if nabbut yar sinner repents.

Then He said; 'A farmer had tweea lads, an' yan on 'em, t'youngomer, sez teu t' aad feller: 'Father, give ez mi sharr ev t' farm, 'at's ta cum ta mi.' An seea he let 'em sharr an' sharr alike.

Nut manny days efter, t' youngomer githered awl he'd gitten t'gither, an' teuk hizsel off inta foreign parts, an' thar' weeasted his brass i' lowse leevin'. An' when he warred awl, hard times cam' ower t'land he was in, an' he co' ta hey nowt. Seea he went an' hired hizsel, an' his maister sent him inta t' fields ti sarra pigs, an' he'd ha' fain iten t' pig meeat, fer neeabody gev' him owt. Twas than he com' tev his sensis, an' said, 'Hoo manny o' mi father's sarvants hez eneugh an' ta spar', an' Ah se fair hungered. Ah'll away heeame ta mi father, an' Ah'll say, "Father, Ah've sinned agen heaven an' ye, an' Ah's nut fit ta bi coa'd yan o yours. Tak mi on as a sarvant lad."'

Wi' that he gat up an' set off heeame, an' his father spied him cummen' when he was a lang way off, an' he was wheea fer him, an' ran oot ta meet him, an' threw his arms roond his neck an' kissed him, fer he was fain ta see him. An' t' lad said, 'Father, Ah've sinned agen heaven an' dun a gert wrang t' ye an' Ah's nut fit t' bi coa'd a lad ev yours.'

But t' father coa'd sarvants, tellen' 'em ta hurry up an' fetch t' best suit o' cleeas th' cud finnd, an' help him t' don, an' git a ring fer his finger, an' shun fer his feet, an' fetch t' fattest cauf in, an' kill't – 'Sooa ez we may awl it an' bi joyful, Fer mi lad 'at Ah thowt was deead 's alive. We had him lost, but noo he's fun ageean.' An' th' started ta enjoy th'sels.

Noo t'owder lad was oot in t'fields an' as he co' near t' hoose he heeard music an' dancin'. An' coa'en yan ev t' sarvants aside he ast what wez on, an' t' sarvant teld him, 'Thi bruther's cum'd heeame, an' becos he's back seeafe an' soond thi father's kill't t' fat cauf.'

He then went crazy, an' wadn't gang in. Seea his father cam' oot t' tice him, but he pleeaned tev his father, 'Awl t' years o' mi life hev Ah bin like a sarvant, dun awl thoo ast er teld mi, an' yet nivver ez mich ez a lile gooat hez t' gin mi, seea's Ah cud hev a merry neet wi' mi mates. But as seun as this weeastrel co's back, efter squanderen awl thoo gev' him i' lowse livin' an' fancy wimmin, thoo kills t' best stalled cauf fer him.'

But t' father sez tew him; 'Mi lad! Thoo's awlis wi' mi, an' awl Ah hev is thine. It's nobbut reet yan sud mak' merry an' bi joyful; fer thi bruther 'at we thowt was deead's alive. He was lost, an' noo he's fun.'

The following version of the same part of St Luke's Gospel, this time in West Riding dialect, was included in *Tales 'at Jesus Telled*, written by the author and televised by Wilfred Pickles in the BBC *Seeing and Believing* series:

T' Prodigal Lad

Nah, Ah'm bahn to tell thee another tale 'at Jesus telled - An' by the way - Ah 'ope ther's none of yer stuck-up enough to think 'at it's nut reight to tell it i' brooad Yorksher. Doesta knaw 'at Jesus an' t' disciples allus talked wi a Northern accent? Oh, aye, they did. They did that. A Galileean accent, it wor – that's 'ow they recognised Peter when 'e were wahrmin' 'is 'ands bi t' fire, tha knaws. So there's nowt wrong wi' tellin' these tales in a plain an 'omely dialect – cos that's 'ow they were telled i' t' first place.

Now it were some varry stuck-up fowk knawn as Pharisees 'at unknowin'ly got Jesus to tell one of 'is mooast famous tales. Tha sees they'd been grummlin' because Jesus wor spendin' a lot of 'is time talkin' to tax-gatherers and sich-like – fowk at t' Pharisees thowt as common as muck. An' one day Jesus turns to t' Pharisees an' 'e says:

Wilfred Pickles.

'There wor once a well-ter-do farmer 'at 'ad two lads. T' youngest on 'em comes up to 'is fatther an' 'e says: "Fatther, will ta give mi my share o' t' land?" T' farmer must 'a' been ta'en aback bi this: t' deeacent thing is to cahr quiet until thi fatther dees afooare tha starts askin' fer thi legacy. 'Owever, t' fatther thowt 'e'd give t'lad a chonce, see what 'e could do on 'is awn, like. So 'e gev 'im 'is share o' t'land.

Well, would-ta credit it? No sooiner does 'e get 'is 'ands on it than t' lad sells it all, taks all t'brass an' goes off inter forin' parts. An' theeare 'e 'as a grand time, blewin it all in, wi' lots o' mates an' plenty o' fancy-women. 'E stays up till all hours, an' mooast o' t' time 'e's as drunk as a fuzzock.

Aye, but when 'e'd spent all 'is brass, it wor a different tale! 'E'd no mates then, ner lady-friends nawther. An' 'e ended up wi' a bit of a job on a farm lookin after t' pigs. By gum! What a come-dahn fer a Jeewish lad. The' believe ther's nowt muckier ner a pig, tha knaws, does t' Jeews, an' it's agen their Law to 'ave owt to do wi pigs. But even though it sickened 'im off – 'e 'ed ter do it. Ee, an' 'e wor that 'ungry 'e could 'ave getten dahn on 'is 'ands 'an' knees an' etten t'pig-swill.

Then, all of a sudden, t'lad comes to 'is senses. "Ee, Ah am a fooil!" 'e says to issen. "A reight blether-'eead! There's fowk workin' for mi fatther 'at can eyt an' sup to the'r 'eart's content. An' 'ere am I starvin ter deeath! Ah mun go back to mi fatther. Ah s'll say to 'im: "Fatther, Ah've done wrong. Ah'm nooan fit ter be a son o' thine. . . Gi'e us a job as one o' thi farm-workers."

So 'e sets off back 'ooam, an' after monny a weary mile 'e lands up i' regs an' tatters, an wi an empty belly. But a long while afooare 'e gets ter t' farm 'is fatther sees 'im, an' instead o' goin' off 'at t' deep end 'e rushes aht to meet 'im, thraws 'is arms rahnd t' lad an' kisses 'im – 'e felt that sorry for 'im, tha sees, an' that glad to see 'im back 'ooame.

T' poor lad starts t'speech 'at 'e'd re'earsed: "Fatther, Ah've done wrong. Ah'm nooan fit to be a son o' thine'– " But 'is fatther butts in, an' calls aht to t' servants: "Come on! Frame yersens! This lad's frozzen aht 'ere. Bring 'im summat ter weear – bring 'im mi top-coit, mi Sunda'-best . . . An' 'es nowt on 'is feet. Bring 'im a pair o booits . . . An' kill yon cawf i' t' mistal – t' one 'at we've been fettenin' up. Wi mun 'ave a celebration. Ah thowt this lad o' mine wor deead, an' 'e's alive ageean! Ah thowt 'e wor lost, an' 'e's come back 'ooame!'

An' soon they were 'evin' a proper 'ooame-coming, with food, an' mewsic, an' dancin'. It wor a reight good do, Ah'll tell thi.

But t' lad's owder brother wor still workin' aht it t' fields. A't end o' t' day, when 'e got near t' 'ahse, 'e 'eard mewsic an' dancin'. 'E says ter t' servants: "What's up? What's all t'celebrations abaht?" "It's thi' brutther," they answer. "'e's come back 'ooame, an' thi fatther's as pleased as Punch, cos 'e's nut come to onny 'arm."

But t' elder brother wor feeurious. An' 'e stood theeare i' t' yard, sulkin' away, an' refeeusin to go in. In a bit, 'is fatther come aht to 'im, an' started pleadin' wi 'im ter come in, an' stop bein' such a jealous mawk.

"Nay, fatther", says t'lad, "Ah've slaved fo' thi all these years. Ah've worked mi' fingers to t' booan, an' Ah've nivver done owt to upset thi. But tha's nut gi'en me even so much as a bit o' gooat-meat so Ah could thraw a party fer mi' mates. But as sooin as this son o' thine turns up, after chuckin' all that brass dahn t'drain, an' livin' wi fancy-women – tha gooas an' kills t' fetted cawf fer 'im!"

"Nay, lad," says t' fatther. "Tha's allus been one o' t' family – an' tha can 'ave owt tha wants – But today's summat special. We couldn't *but* mak a bit of a fuss. Wi thowt this brother o' thine wor deead – an' 'e's alive ageean! We thowt 'e wor lost – an' 'e's come back 'ooame!"

A selection of dialect prose would not be complete without a few examples of humorous Yorkshire anecdotes. Some of these are very much alive, constantly going the rounds in after-dinner speeches and so forth. A few contain real dialect, an understanding of which is essential for the comic effect – as in the case of the first example below, which is meaningless to anyone not familiar with the North Riding pronunciation of 'How?'

A little lad went into the village shop to order something, saying 'Mi feyther sent mi.' The shopkeeper, not recognising him, asked in standard English, 'Who is your father?'

'E's nobbut dowly', replied the lad.

Two old Yorkshire chaps, about to pass each other in the street, hesitated, thinking that they recognised each other. Realising they were both mistaken, one of them said: 'Well, Ah'll bi blowed! Ah thowt it wor thee – an' tha thowt it wor me . . . an' bi gow! It's nawther on us!'

Sydney Martin of York tells the story of a farmer friend who had a large pocket watch which fascinated his little grandson. One day as he was rubbing the face of the watch he said to the boy: 'This is thine when owt 'appens to me.'

Ever afterwards, when he came to see him, the little boy would rush in through the door shouting: 'Owt 'appened, Grandad?'

A miner, late for the day shift, was getting dressed in a hurry.

'Nay,' said his nagging wife, 'tha's putten thi clogs on t' wrong feet.'

'Ah knaw', said the miner. 'They ought ter be on thine!'

A true story from the Keighley area in the twenties was told by a doctor who visited an old farmer who was dying. Having found no perceptible pulse he said to the wife:

'I fear that poor John has passed away'.

'Nay, doctor,' said a feeble voice from the bed, 'Ah ammot deead yet!'

The old wife turned to her husband and said: 'Thee 'od thi tongue, lad. T' doctor knaws better ner thee!'

A teacher had told her class in the Dales the parable of the shepherd who went looking for a lost sheep, leaving the ninety-nine others in the fold. Why did he look for this one sheep, she asked, when he had so many others?

A little boy's hand shot up. 'Please, Miss,' he said. 'Appen it wor t' tup.'

Two little lads were looking at a statue under which was the inscription 'Sir Titus Salt, Bart'.

What does 'Bart' mean?' asked one. The other looked up at the statue and said, 'Baht 'at, o' course!'

'Thoo's getten poison i' thi' sistren, that's why thoo's bellywark,' says t' docther. 'Thoo mun a thi teeath oot'.

'What?' Ah says, 'All on 'em?'

'Aye' he says. 'ivvery yan' . . . So Ah took 'em oot, an laad em on t'table.

There are several jokes about Yorkshire farmers watering down their milk, including the story of the woman who asked for milk in one pail and 't' watter in t' other' so she could mix her own. Then there was the lad who used to shout out every time he saw a certain farmer, 'Tha watters thi milk, tha knaws!' The farmer complained to the lad's teacher and father, who told him he must on no account say this again. Next time he saw the farmer the lad simply called out: 'Tha knaws!'

A notice put up on a gate at Duck Bridge near Danby ran as follows:

> Ye'll know which is t' bull
> Bi t' ring in 'is snoot:
> Seea deeant stand 'n gawp –
> It's taame ti git oot!

'Hah monny is ther' 'at works at t' Tahn 'All?'
'Oh, abaht 'awf on 'em.'

One of the great Yorkshire traditions is the local brass or silver band, sustained by the loyalty of long-serving players. Ernest, who had played the tenor horn with a famous brass band for fifty years decided it was time he retired. When the conductor announced this at a rehearsal, a voice from the back shouted: 'What's up, Ernest? Can't ta settle?'

A man whose wife had died went to see the monumental mason in his Yorkshire town requesting him to carve on her headstone, 'Lord, she was thine'.

When he visited the graveyard he saw that the inscription read: 'Lord, she was thin.'

Very annoyed, he went back to the mason and said. 'Nay, tha's med a reight mullock on it. Tha's gone an' left t' 'e' off!'

'Oh, dearie me!' said the mason 'Dooan't thee fret thissen, lad. Ah'll mak it reight fer thi.'

The next time the man saw the gravestone it read: 'Ee, Lord, she was thin.'

From the newsletter of the East Riding Dialect Society comes this conversation which makes an appropriate point:

Lass: Wheer's thoo off teea?
Lad: Meeatin at Driffil (Driffield)
Lass: What sooart ov a meetin?
Lad: Charlie's gannin wi ma. We're off to listen to fowk talkin' i' dialect.
Lass: An 'oo much is that off ti cost tha?
Lad: Wah, t' meeatin's free. Aboot three pund for petrol.
Lass: Gi' ma yan o' them punds an' Ah'll talk dialect ti tha all neet . . . Tha'll save a couple o' pund, an' all!

Yorkshire Dialect Verse

Verse in Yorkshire vernacular can be found in some of our earliest literature – in the medieval mystery plays of York and Wakefield, for example. The writing of individual poems in Yorkshire dialect has a long tradition going back to at least the early part of the eighteenth century ranging from such pieces as the old, atmospheric ballad **A Dree Neet** to the following, the first stanza of a song from Henry Carey's ballad-opera **A Wonder, or an Honest Yorkshireman** (1736) later transposed into NR dialect:

> Ah is, i' truth, a coontry youth
> Neean used teea Lunnon fashions;
> Yet vartue guides, an still presides,
> Ower all mah steps an' passions.
> Neea coortly leear, bud all sincere,
> Neea bribe shall ivver blinnd me;
> If thoo can like a Yorksher tike,
> A rooague thoo'll nivver finnd me.

There were other songs and poems, such as *I'm Yorkshire too, The Yorkshire Horse Dealers, A Wensleydale lad* and five by the Rev Thomas Browne (died 1798) who was editor of the *Hull Advertiser*.

Yorkshire's first known worker-poet was David Lewis of Knaresborough. He was a self-educated farmer, later schoolmaster, who in 1815 published *The Landscape*, a collection of his poems in standard English, with two in local dialect. His **Elegy on the death of a Frog** clearly shows the influence of the great pioneer of dialect writing, Robert Burns, especially in his poem *To a Mouse*. Like Burns, this farmer too has come across a poor creature on whom he philosophises, only in this case the frog has been accidentally killed by the scythe, and David Lewis speaks to it, as Burns spoke to the mouse:

Poor luckless frog, why com thoo here?
Thoo sure were destitute o' fear;
Some other way could thoo nut steer
    To shun the grass?
For noo that life, which all hod dear,
    Is gean, alas!

Later in the poem he meditates on the fact that we all must soon be cut down by the scythe of time, even pretty girls:

Ye bonnie lasses, livin' flooers,
Of cottage mean, or gilded booers,
Possessèd of attractive pooers,
    Ye all mun gang
Like frogs in meadows fed bi shooers
    Ere owt be lang

Even earlier, in 1808, David Lewis had published the following poem, based on a true incident, about a young chimney sweep whose soot-blackened face scares away thieves:

The Sweeper and the Thieves

A sweeper's lad was late o' t' neet,
His slape-shod shun had leeam'd his feet;
He call'd ti see a good awd deeame,
'At monny a time had trigg'd his wame,
For he wor then fahve miles fra yam:
He ax'd i' t' lair ti let him sleep,
An' he'd next day, ther chimlers sweep.
They supper'd him wi' country fare,
Then show'd him tul his hooal i' t' lair.
He crept intul his streay bed,
His poak o' seeat beneath his heead;
He wor content, nur car'd a pin,
An' his good frind then lock'd him in.
The lair fra t' hoose a distance stood,
Between 'em grew a lahtle wood:

Aboot midneet, or nearer moorn,
Two thieves brak in ti steeal ther coorn;
Heving a leet i' lantern dark,
They seean ti winder fell ti wark;
And wishin' they'd a lad to fill,
Young Brush (wheea yet had ligg'd quite still)
Thinkin' 'at t' men belang'd ti t' hoose
An' that he noo mud be of use,
Jump'd doon directly on ti t' fleear –
An' t' thieves then beath ran oot o' t' deear,
Nor stopt at owt, nur thin, nur thick,
Fully convinc'd it wor awd Nick.
The sweeper lad then ran reet seean
Ti t'hoose, an' tell'd 'em what wor deean:
Maister an' men then quickly raise,
An' ran ti t' lair wi' hoaf ther clais.
Twea horses, secks, an' leet they fand,
Which had been left by t' thievish band;
These roond i' t' neybourheead they cry'd
But nut an awner e'er apply'd,
For neean durst horses awn, or secks,
They wor se freeten'd o' ther necks;
Yan horse an' seck wor judg'd t' sweeper's share,
Because he kept t' farmer's coorn an' lair.

The subject matter of early dialect poets was not necessarily rural. Here is part of the **Sheffield Cutler's Song**, written by Abel Bywater in about 1830. It concerns men forging knives known as flat-backs, about to slake their thirst at the 'penny hop', a dance at the local pub:

Coom all you cutlin' heroes, where'ersome 'er you be
All you what works at flat-backs, coom listen unto me;
    A basketful for a shillin'
    To mak 'em we are willin',
Or swap 'em for red herrin's, aar bellies to be fillin'
Or swap 'em for red herrin's, aar bellies to be fillin'. . .

Let's send for a pitcher o' ale, lad, for Ah'm gerrin'
varry droy,
Ah'm ommost chok'd wi' smithy sleck, the wind it is so
hoigh.
    Gie Rafe an' Jer a drop,
    They sen they cannot stop,
They're i' sich a moighty hurry to get to t' penny hop,
They're i' sich a moighty hurry to get to t' penny hop.

North Yorkshire's best-known early poet was John Castillo,
born in Ireland, but from the age of three brought up at
Lealholm Bridge, ten miles or so west of Whitby. A stone-
mason, he was converted under Methodism and became a
local preacher. Before he learnt to read and write he composed
Awd Isaac, which he dictated to Joseph Smith and published
at Northallerton in 1832. It is a long poem of thirty stanzas in
the Bilsdale dialect describing how 'Yah neet, as Ah went
heeam fra wark' the narrator meets Awd Isaac who tells him
his life story. Here are the closing stanzas, the last being carved
on Castillo's tombstone:

Oft hev Ah lang'd yon hill ti clim,
Ti hev a bit mare prooase wi' him
Wheas coonsel like a pleeasin dreeam,
    Is deear ti me;
Sin' roond the warld sike men as he
    Seea few ther be.

Corrupted bewks he did detest,
For his wur ov the varry best;
This meead him wiser than the rest
    O' t' neeaburs roond,
Tho' poor i' purse, wi' senses blest
    An' judgment soond.

Befoore the silvery neet ov age,
The precepts ov the sacred page
His meditation did engage,
    That race ti run;
Like thooase, who 'spite o' Satan's rage,
    The prahze hed won.

Bud noo his een 's geean dim i' deeath,
Neea mare a pilgrim here on eearth,
His sowl flits fra' her shell beneeath,
    Ti reealms o' day,
Whoor carpin care, an' pain, an' deeath,
    Are deean away.

Samuel Laycock (1825-93) was born in Marsden, only a couple of miles this side of the border with Lancashire, and although our friends in that county think of him as one of their own poets, we will quote just the first and last stanzas of his **Welcome, bonny Brid** (bird), which is about a baby born into the poverty so well known to the poet and his fellow textile workers:

Tha'rt welcome, little bonny brid,
But shouldn't ha' come just when tha did;
Toimes are bed.
We're short o' pobbies for eawr Joe,
But that, of course, tha didn't know,
Did ta, lad? . . .

But tho we've childer two or three
We'll mak a bit o' reeawm for thee,
Bless thee lad!
Th'art th' prettiest brid we have i' th' nest
So hutch up closer to mi breast:
Aw'm thi dad.

John Hartley.

The most prolific writer of Yorkshire dialect, both in prose and verse, was John Hartley of Halifax (1839-1915), synonymous with *The Clock Almanac*, where his poems were first published. He was a lively, somewhat bohemian character, living in Leeds, Bradford and London as well as Halifax, and visiting America soon after the Civil War. He was an acute observer of the poverty in the industrial towns of the West Riding, as is illustrated by **Bite Bigger**, the first poem he wrote and recited at the Beacon Club, which met in the Corporation Arms, Halifax. It concerns a poor lad who finds an apple in the gutter and offers the first bite to little Billy, aged five, to whom he says: 'Nay, tha hasn't taen much. Bite ageean, an' bite bigger, nah do!' The poet concludes by praising the innate kindness of the poor:

> God bless thi! do just as tha will,
> An' may better days speedily come;
> Tho' clamm'd, an' hauf donn'd, mi lad, still
> Tha'rt a deal nearer Heaven nur some.

John Hartley's love of children, even though sometimes sentimentally expressed, is a common theme, as in this poem about his donation of a halfpenny:

A Hawpo'th

> Whear is thi Daddy, doy? Whear is thi mam?
> What are ta cryin' for, poor little lamb?
> Dry up thi peepies, pet, wipe thi weet face;
> Tears on thy little cheeks seem aht o' place.
> What do they call thi, lad? Tell me thi name;
> Have they been ooinin thi? Why, it's a shame!
> Here, tak this hawpny, an buy thi some spice,
> Rocksticks or humbugs or summat 'at's nice.
> Then run off hooam ageean, fast as tha can;
> Thear – tha'rt all reight ageean; run like a man.
> He wiped up his tears wi' his little white brat,
> An he tried to say summat, Ah couldn't tell what:
> But his little face breeten'd wi' pleasure all throo:
> Eh! – it's cappin, sometimes, what a hawpny can do.

Hartley's verse covers a wide range of topics, including love poems such as this:

Nelly o' Bobs

Who is it 'at lives i' that cot on the lea?
Joy o' mi heart, an leet o' mi ee;
Who is that lass at's sooa dear unto me?
   Nelly o' Bob's o' t' Crowtrees.

Who is it goes trippin ower dew-spangled grass,
Singin sooa sweetly? Shoo smiles as Ah pass;
Bonniest, rooasy-cheek'd, gay-hearted lass!
   Nelly o' Bob's o' t' Crowtrees.

Who is it Ah see i' mi dreeams ov a neet?
Who lovinly whispers words tender an sweet
Till Ah wakken to finnd 'at shoo's noawhear i' t' seet?
   Nelly o' Bob's o' t' Crowtrees.

Who is it 'at leeads me sooa lively a donce,
Yet to talk serious ne'er gi'es me a chonce,
An nivver replied when Ah begged on her once?
   Nelly o' Bob's o' t' Crowtrees.

Who is it ivvery chap's hank'rin to get,
Yet tosses her heead an flies off in a pet;
As mich as to say, 'Yo've net getten me yet?'
   Nelly o' Bob's o' t' Crowtrees.

Who is it could mak life a long summer's day,
Whose smile wod drive sorrow an trouble away,
An mak t' hardest wark, if for her, seem like play?
   Nelly o' Bob's o' t' Crowtrees.

Who is it Ah'll have if Ah've ivver a wife,
An love her, her only, to t' end o' mi life,
An nurse her i' sickness, an guard her from strife?
   Nelly o' Bob's o' t' Crowtrees.

Who is it 'at's promised, to-neet, if it's fine,
To meet me at t' corner o' t' mistal at nine?
Why, its her 'at Ah've langed for sooa long to mak mine,
　　Nelly o' Bobs o' t' Crowtrees.

One of John Hartley's comic poems, **Ahr Mary's Bonnet**, became so popular as a recitation piece that many Yorkshire people knew it by heart (and some still do), with the result that all kinds of variations have appeared, including a South Yorkshire version called *Ahr Sal's new Bonnet*. Here is how it was recited in the Bradford area until at least the 1940s:

Ahr Mary's Bonnet

Es-ta seen ahr Mary's bonnet?
It's a stunner an' nooa mistak!
Yoller ribbons, yoller rooases,
An' a gurt big feather dahn t' back;
Ah Mary went ter chu'ch last Sunda:
T' congregation did nowt but stare;
T' parson says, 'This is nut a flahr-show,
But a house of prayer;'
Ahr Mary says: 'Thy 'eead's bald,
Nowt in it, ner nowt on it:
Would-ta like a feather aht o' t' back o' my bonnet?'

Another dialect worker-poet, this time a Nidderdale lead-miner, was Thomas Blackah (1828-95). Born on Greenhow Hill near Pateley Bridge, he wrote and published *T' Nidderdill Olminac* and various poems with local subjects, such as the following:

Pateley Reeaces

Attention all, baith great an' small,
  An dooan't screw up yer feeaces;
While I rehearse, i' simple verse,
  A coont o' Pateley Reeaces.

Fra all ower t' moors, they com bi scoores
  Girt skelpin' lads an' lasses;
An' cats an' dogs, an' coos an' hogs,
  An' hosses, mules, an' asses.

Oade foaks wer thar, fra near an' far
  At cuddant fairly hopple;
An' laughin' brats, as wild as cats,
  Ower heeads an' heels did topple.

The Darley lads, arrived i' squads,
  Wi' smiles all ower ther feeaces,
An' Hartwith youths, wi' screw'd-up mooths
  In wonder watch'd the reeaces.

Fra Menwith Hill, and Folly Gill,
  Thorntyat, an' Deacre Paster,
Fra Thruscross Green, an' t'Heets wer seen
  Croods cumin' thick an' faster.

'Tween Bardin Brigg and Threshfield Rig
  Oade Wharfedeeale gat a thinnin';
An' Gerston plods laid heavy odds
  On Creeaven Lass fer winnin'.

Sich lots were seen o' Hebdin Green,
  Ready seean on i' t' mornin',
While Aptrick chaps, i' carts an' traps,
  Wer off ta Patela' spornin.

All Greenho' Hill, past Coadsteeanes kill,
  Com toltherin' an singin'
Harcastle coves, like sheep i' droves,
  Oade Palmer Simp wer bringin'.

Baith short an' tall, past Gowthit Halll,
  T' up-deealers kept on steerin',
For ne'er before, roond Middlesmoor,
  Had ther been sich a clearin'.

All kinds and sorts o' games an' sports
  Had t' Patela' chaps pervided,
An' weel did t' few, ther business do,
  At ower 'em persided.

'Twad tak a swell a munth ta tell
  All t' ins an' oots o' t' reeaces.
Hoo far the' ran, which hosses wan,
  An' which wer' back'd for pleeaces . . .

An' when at last the sports were past,
  All heeamward turn'd ther feeaces;
Ta ne'er relent at e'er the' spent
  A day wi' Patela' Reeaces.

Bill o' th' Hoylus End was the pen-name of William Wright (1836-97), a warp-dresser who published the *Haworth, Cowenhead and Bogthorne Original Almanack*. One of his poems testifies to the anguish caused by the death of a child, so common in Victorian times:

Cowd as Leead

An' arta fra thi fatther torn
So early i' thi youthful morn,
An mun Ah pine away forlorn
I' grief an' pain?   .
For consolashun Ah sall scorn
If tha be ta'en.

Oh, yes, tha art, an' Ah mun wail
Thi loss through ivvery hill an' dale,
Fer nah it is too true a tale,
Tha'rt cowd as leead.
An' nah thi bonny face is pale,
Tha'rt deead! Tha'rt deead!

Ah miss tha when Ah cum fra t' shop,
An' see thi bat, an' ball, an top;
An' Ah's be ommost fit ta drop,
Ah sall so freeat;
An' Oh! Mi varry heart may stop
An' cease to beeat!

Ah allus aimed, if tha'd been spared,
Of summat better to hev shared,
Ner what thi poor owd father fared,
I' this cowd sphere;
Yet, after all, Ah s't nooan 'a' cared
If tha'd stayed here.

But O! Tha Conqueror Divine,
'At vanquished deeath i' Palestine,
Tak to thi arms this lad o' mine –
Nooan freely given;
But mak him same as wun o' thine
Wi' Thee i' Heaven.

The twentieth century has produced a number of Yorkshire dialect poets, of which a small selection is now given. The one who most clearly followed in the footsteps of dialect worker-poets was Fred Brown (1893–1980). Born in Keighley he grew up in Huddersfield, and worked in textile mills for over fifty years.

Safety First

Ther's summat up wi' t' chimney
T' Inspector's been to t' stack,
He's squinted up at t' plaistering,
An' fun' a gaping crack.

They'll soon be bringing t' ladders
T' scaffold-poles and ropes,
And scrimming up like monkeys
On' t' overhanging copes.

They'll be chipping now, and pointing
Full throng for monny a week,
And cursing down at t' firer-up,
For makking too much reek:

They'll then pull down their ladders,
And cart away the'r poles,
While we go on wi' t' weyving,
As safe as burrowed moles.

Fred Brown WR

Not for viewing

If there wor winders i hearts,
An fan-leets i mahnds,
What sales there'd be
For curtains an blahnds!

Fred Brown WR

A Hoss

A hoss is t' nicest thing Ah knaw;
It nivver answers back;
It pulls gurt looads, does a'most owt,
If nobbut yer've got t' knack.

Ah like ter feel one muzzle up
An' let me pat it heead.
Yer'd a'most thowt it thenked me fo'
A little bit o' breead.

Ah offen ride on Oldroyd's mare,
Shoo's big an' strong an' brooad,
An' Ah'm reight prahd o' Bessie when
Shoo clop, clop, clops up t' rooad.

A hoss he's got more sense ner fowk –
An' whippin' 'em is mean,
It's t' hoss's feelin's what they hurt –
Ah've seen it i' the'r een.

Will Clemence ('Young Fred') WR

Ah'm Comin' Back . . .

Ah'm comin back, Ah'm stalled o' t' leets;
    Ah'm sick to deeath o' city streets;
An t' city's ways Ah's nivver leearn,
    Ah'm coming back to t' hills ageean.
Ah'm comin back, there's nowt else fo't
    Mi belly warks wi this mad lot,
Ah'm comin back to t' wind on t' fells,
    To t' cotton-grass an t' heather-bells.
Ah'm comin back, mi thost to sleck
    I' t' peeaty wine o' t' Ewden Beck,
Mi heart to wahrm, mi sowl to fill
    Wi t' seet o' t' stars thro Hartcliff Hill. . .

Gordon Allen North WR

T' Hoss Blinnders

Ah seed t' hoss blinnders hung in t' stable theer –
   Dusty an' dowly, same as summat felled –
Nivver i' use Ah s' think these monny years,
   Since tractors come, an' t' hosses all was selled.

Yance, oot at work in t' fields in t' wind an' t' sun –
   Warm wi' hoss sweeat, yon brokken bit champed breet –
Noo, t' blinnders is but kelterment, worth nowt;
   Wi' tractors here, there's not yah hoss i' seet.

Kathleen Stark ER

A Lovely Lass is Shoo

Ah took her i mi airms today,
   A lovely lass is shoo;
Ah kussed her, an shoo bad me stay
   An stroke her achin broo;
Her skin's as snod as glass itsen,
   Her lips are honey-sweet:
Oh, what new wo'lds 'll oppen when
   Shoo's i mi airms toneet?

Gordon Allen North WR

Epitaph for a Countryman

Thoo's warked for lang eneeaf – noo bide i peace
I' t' chotch-garth ere, bi t' fields thoo kept si weel;
Cum spring, thi coos an cauves 'll graze nigh-and,
An t'soil thoo luved, i sleep 'll be thi seal.

O' field an forest noo for fifty yeear
Neea yan cud stack or theeak or fell a tree,
Snig, slash, maw, milk, drahve osses or guide t'pleeaf,
Dig drains or lig a hedge as weel as thee.

Lang sin thoo bowled for t'village creckit team,
Knocked runs, scored goals, wan monny a runnin prize;
Life's innins ower'd noo, rist quiet a whahl
They'll likelins need thy help i Paradise!

Bill Cowley NR

New Born

A caud wet neet is all ther is ti welcome thee,
Bud muther's here, nuzzling an tryin ti clean thee up.
Her tahm o waitin's gitten ower at last,
An noo she thinks o nowt bud thee, her lahtle tup.
Fer ivvery tahm thoo bleats, she's quickly bah thi side
Makin a few soft mutterin noises of her awn,
An if thoo's feelin hungry, lets thoo in ti sup
Her sweet warm milk, reet good fer things at's newly born.
Wi tummy full, thoo's settled doon, all cumfy noo,
An snuggled up besahde thi mum, thoo's keepin wahrm.
She's picked mooast sheltered spot in t' field, near t' dry
    steeane wall,
An theer fer t' rist o' t' neet she keeps thi safe fra harm.
Seun as t' sun pooakes its watery heead ower t' brow o' t' hill
Thoo's up on wobbly legs an tryin ti walk aroond.
Thoo'd lahke ti gan alang an reeace wi t other lambs,
An in a day or twa, thoo will an all, Ah's boond.
Noo t' shepherd cums along, an finnds thoo beeath alreet,
He's capped at thoo's a tup, good size an colour too.
'Thoo's gitten yan o t' grandest muthers i mi flock',
He sez, 'Ah wish at all mi lambs wer grand as thoo'.

Ruth Dent NR

Knaw Nowt

Yan o' t' sayings of old wad be
'Knaw nowt, mi lad, knaw nowt.
Whativver question thoo gits axed,
Knaw nowt, mi lad, knaw nowt.'

When his lad went off ti skeeal
An browt yam his repoort,
Fayther seeamed a bit upset
An sent skeeal boss a nooat.

'Thoo's nut deean ower weeal' said Dad,
'Nut as weeal as Ah'd a thowt.'
Seea t' lad replied 'Thoo allus said
"Knaw nowt, mi lad, knaw nowt!"'

Sydney Martin ER (York)

Cawd Feeat

Awd Faarmer Ben, 'e teeak a wife,
A sthrappin woman, Maude,
A willin lass – wi' just yah fault –
'Er feeat was allus cawd.

Whahle other fooalk, i' summer tahm
'ed waarmish feeat, tha foond,
Wi' poor Maude's icy pasties
It was winther ahll t' yeear roond.

Yan was just as cawd as t'other:
Ther was, upon mi wodd,
A deeal mair caarcilaation
Iv a pund o' frozz'n cod.

Wen Ben fosst felt 'is missus feeat
That icy cawd 'n raw,
'Ah'd seeaner 'ev 'em sweeat,' 'e shoots,
'Than feeal lahke lumps o' snaw.'

'Ah've nivver felt owt as cawd,' ses 'e
'Sin a yeear last Kessmass tonn'd,
That neet Ah walked fre' t' 'Are 'n 'Oonds
Sthraight inti Chulton pond.'

Bud cum yah neet Ben gans upstairs
When t' clock showed it was tahm,
An seean 'aard fast asleeap 'e was
Fair snuggled doon 'n waarm.

Then Maude cums creeapin up ti bed,
An wiv a sudden smack
Sha claps 'er icy plaates o' meeat
I' small o' t' faarmer's back.

Poor Ben, 'e lowps cleean oot o' bed,
As cawd sthruck 'im full seean.
'e thowt fer shewer 'e mun be back
I' Chulton pond ageean.

'Daft lass, thoo's snaarled mi innards up,'
'e tells 'er wiv a rooar,
Then clicked sum 'appin' off 'n bed
An ligg'd 'issen o' t' floor.

Bud t' floor waan't reet fer 'im 'e fun',
An felt as 'aard as stooane;
'e cudn't get a wink o' sleeap
An ached in ivvry booane.

Wi' t' faarmer aachin', staarved 'n sooar,
'Enow,' 'e mooans, 'Ah's beeat,'
An was glad ti crawl back inti bed
Ti Maude 'n 'er cawd feeat.

Bud when 'lectric blankets fosst cem oot
T' awd faarmer bowt yan fast;
Ses 'Cum, Maude. Get thi feeat o' yon –
An tonn thing up – full blast.'

Sooa noo Maude keeaps 'er feeat waarm
Wi' blanket scorrchin' red –
Whahle t' faarmer's sweeatin' lahke a bull –
Wi' *is* feeat oot o' bed.

Geoff M Robinson ER

Christmas Crackers

Come, lads and lasses, frame yersens!
We'r bahn ter t' Christmas Crack,
Fer tales an' poims in t' Yorksher tongue,
As wi' tu'n wer clocks all back
Ter t' days o' wer youth, an' t' days o' yore,
An' fu'ther back still ter long afooare,
When t' stars shone dahn yon neet
On t' dawnin o' treeuth an' leet
In a bit of a mistal wi muck all rahnd –
An' theeare in t' midst yon shepherds fahnd
T' babby in 'ippins all wahrmly lapped,
An t' three Wise Men, all on 'em capped
At such a gloorious seet!

Nay, we'r not same as fowk tha sees terday,
Spendin the'r brass wi' Christmas greed . . .
Wi s'll think o' t' meanin o' yon grand day –
An' think of *all* t' childer born i' need –
Wi s'll do t' job right – an' then wi s'll mak
This year's Christmas really crack!
For liftin low sperrits ther's no fowk can whack us:
We'r baht comic 'ats – but we'r reight Christmas Crackers!

Arnold Kellett WR

T' White Rooase O' Yorksher

T' White Rooase o' Yorksher,
By gum, it looks grand!
Sin t' day it wor plucked
Bi yon royal 'and
It's been wer awn emblem,
An' worn wi real pride –
Sin' Richard Plantag'net
Picked fust Yorksher side!
Aye, then t' Battle o' Towton,
When t' beck ran wi blood,
An' yon poor Lancastrians
Wor fettled fer good –
Nay, we dooan't grudge 'em *their* rooase,
It's a fine gradely red,
But on t' reight side o' t' Pennines
Ahr flahrs are peeure-bred:
It's rare is a white un,
You dooan't see 'em that oft . . .
Same as snaw-drifts – or virgins,
All scented an' soft –
But if fowk tak advantage,
An we're badly tret,
Well, we're nut baht sharp thorns
'At they'll nooan ferget . . .
Aye, we're tough 'ere i' Yorksher,
An prahd o' wer past:
Yon three ancient Ridin's
Fer ivver will last!
Tak no 'eed o' t' gaffers
Wi the'r moitherin plans;
Blood's thicker ner watter –
An' a gatherin' o' t' clans
Is just what we need, lad,
Fer reightin' all t' wrongs . . .

It's a champion thing
Ter feel tha belongs!
So come, Yorkshire Tykes, then,
An' moisten thi throit
Wi a tooast ter t' Brooad Acres,
An' in thi best coit,
Or thi bonniest clooathes,
Stand up fer Yorksher,
An' don a White Rooase!
It's nobbut t' off-comed-uns
'At dooan't understand:
Ee . . . t' White Rooase o' Yorksher –
By gum, it looks grand!

                        Arnold Kellett WR

YORKSHIRE DICTIONARY

Words which differ from standard English only in a vowel change (eg **abaht/aboot, booits/beeats** etc) have been excluded in order to make room for less common and more interesting words. For details of patterns of spelling and pronunciation see pages 25–33, 47, 50.

Although all these words occur in Yorkshire dialect some are used in other areas, especially Scotland. Words not appearing here may be found in word-lists for particular localities, trades, crafts etc, or in the *English Dialect Dictionary* by Joseph Wright.

aboon above
addle to earn
afeeared afraid
afooare before
agate going, started, busy
ageean, agin again; against, opposite
aiblins hardly, perhaps NER
'aigs haws
alicker (see **elicker**)
'allack (see **hallack**)
'allidas holidays
allus always
ammot am not
anent, anenst next to, opposite
'an'kercher handkerchief
apiece each
'appen perhaps
'appins (see **happins**)
'ard on fast asleep
'ardlins hardly
arran spider
arse-pocket back pocket
ask(er) newt
ass to ask
assen-'ook ash-pan
asteead instead

'at that
at-after afterwards
attercrop spider
'attock stook, group of sheaves
atwixt between
aud, auld old NER
'avver (see **haver**)
awn (see **own**)
'aw-porth (see **hawporth**)
awther either
aye yes
ax to ask

back'ards-rooad backwards
back back to move (a vehicle) in reverse
back-end autumn
back-endish feeling that summer is over
back-side bottom, posterior
back-word (to give) to cancel
badly ill
bahn going
baht without
bairn child
bakst'n heated stone for baking
balmy (see **barmy**)

band string, rope
band in t' nick (see p 53)
bar except
barfin horse-collar
barguest ghost, evil spirit
barkum (see **barfin**)
barlow truce word (children's games)
barm yeast
barmy crazy
barn child
barry-coit/cooat baby's undergarment
bassock to batter, clatter
baulk beam
bawl to shout; weep
beck stream
beeal to shout; weep NER
beeas(t) cattle
beeastlins (see p 52)
beesom broom
behint, behunt behind
belder to bellow
bellusses bellows
belly stomach, abdomen
belly-button 'oil navel
belly-wark stomach-ache
belong to own; come from
belt to hit hard
beltenger severe blow
benjy man's straw hat
benk bench, seat
bensel WR, **bezzle** NER to beat, thrash
bid to invite (especially to a funeral)
biddy louse
bide to stand, put up with
bield shelter
bink (see **benk**)
black-bright really dirty
black-clock black beetle
blaeberry bilberry
blamed (see **blessed**)

blash wet, squally
bleb blister, spot
blegs blackberries
blessed damned (mild curse)
blether bladder
blether-'eead fool
blether on to talk nonsense
blew blue
blinnders blinkers
blood-alley kind of marble, streaked with red
bobbin-ligger (see p 53)
bobby-dazzler excellent, very smart
bobby-'oil police station
boggart ghost, spirit etc.
bogie home-made go-cart
bon! (see p 55)
bonn to burn NER
boose-stake (see p 52)
boskin (see p 52)
braffin (see **barfin**)
brandrith frame for pans etc
brant steep
brass money
brat apron, pinafore
bray to hammer, hit, beat
breead-fleg (see p 53)
breeaks trousers NER
brek to break
brig bridge
britches trousers
brock badger
broddle to poke, pick out
browt brought
brussen bursting, esp. of over-full stomach; boastful etc
brussen-gutted greedy
brussen-guts glutton
brust burst
bub to drink (esp of children)
buck cheek
buck-stick cheeky person, esp child

bud but
budget large can for milk
buffit small, low stool
bull'eeads tadpoles
bummel-kite blackberry
bun bound, certain
bust to burst
buzzard moth
by gow! by God! good Lord!
by gum! my word! fancy that!
byre cowshed

cack-'anded left-handed, clumsy
cah-clap patch of cow dung WR
cahr to stay (quiet etc)
call (see **kall**)
cam bank, slope
canned drunk
cannle candle
cap to surprise, astonish; beat,
  surpass
carse cake brown bread
cast (see **rig-welted**)
catie-cornered aslant, cock-eyed
catty (see **piggy**)
caus'a' causeway, pavement
cauve to calve
cawf calf
cawf-licked hair sticking up
cham(b)er bedroom
champion excellent,
  outstandingly good
charver mate, lad
chats small potatoes fried whole
chelp to chatter, talk loudly
childer children
chimla chimney
chimley chimney
chippy starling
chonce chance
chonce 'un illegitimate child
choose-'ow no matter how,
  whatever happens
chuffed pleased

chump piece of wood; fool
chump to collect wood for
  bonfires (see p 76)
chunter to grumble, mutter
cinders coke
claht clout, hit WR
claht cloth (e.g. **dish claht**) WR
claht-'eead fool
clais clothes NR
clammed (see **clemmed**)
clap cow dung
clap-cowd cold (esp of food)
clart to smear
clartment flattery, hypocrisy
clarty dirty; sticky
clashy windy and wet NR
cleeas clothes NER
cleat coltsfoot
cleg horse-fly
clemmed parched with thirst;
  starving
clemmy stone
cletch family of young (children)
click to catch; become friends
clock beetle
clog ageean to recover
  (see p 63)
cloise enclosure, field
clomp to tread heavily
closit outside toilet; walk-in
  cupboard
clout cloth
cod pod
cod to kid, deceive
coil-leader coalman
collops thick slices; fried
  potatoes
conny neat, nice etc
cop to catch
cowk core (of apple)
crack friendly conversation
crake crow
crammly tottery
cratch wooden fireside chair

creeak to creak, croak; crow NER
creeaked crooked
creel (see p 53)
crewkt crooked
crozzle to wrinkle, wither etc
cuddy donkey; hedge sparrow NER
cuddy-'anded left-handed NER
cuddy-wifter left-handed person NER
curn currant
cush up! here! (to cows)
cut canal

daft silly, foolish
dawks hands
daytal (see p 52)
dee to die
deeaf deaf WR
deeaf dough NER
deear door NER
deg to sprinkle
delf quarry
delf-rack plate-rack (on wall)
deng damn (mild curse)
despert very, extremely ER
ding to throw, knock
dobby a pot marble
doff take off
doffer (see p 53)
doit (see p 63)
dollop lump of something soft
dolly tub (see p 53)
don put on
dooaf dough WR
dooar-'oil doorway
dooar-st'n doorstep
dother to dirty
dowly gloomy, miserable; ill
dowter daughter
doy dear, darling
drat damn (see p 55-6)
dree wearisome, melancholy

drinkins (see p 53)
druffen drunk
dub puddle WR
dursn't dare not

'eart-sluffened heart-broken
'eck! (see **heck!**)
ee, een eye, eyes
'eeam (see **heeam**)
eeasin eaves
eldrin kindling
elicker vinegar
emmot ant
'engments! (see **hengments!**)
enow enough
'es-ta? have you?
etten eaten
eyt to eat

faddy fussy, particular etc
fahl ugly, grim-looking
fain very pleased (to)
fair really, completely
fairish considerable NER
fan found
fashion (to) to bring oneself to
fast short (of), stuck (for) etc
fatty-cakes small sweet pastry-like cakes WR
feeast local fair, annual holiday
fent remnant of cloth
ferrie (see **foggie**)
fettle to fix, deal with, prepare, clean etc
fettle condition
fettlin day cleaning day, usually Friday
feyt to fight
firepoint poker
flags (see **flegs**)
flaid frightened
flay to frighten
flay-creeak, flay-crow scarecrow

flaysome terrifying
fleet floor; inner room
flegs, flegstooanes paving or floor stones
flig to fly
flit to move house
flittermouse bat
flooer flower; flour NER
fluff to break wind silently WR
fluffin frumenty (qv) made with barley
flummox to bewilder, confuse
fog (see p 78)
foggie first (children's games)
foisty musty, mouldy etc.
fond foolish
fooaks people NER
fooarced certain (see p 63)
for all in spite of the fact
forenooin drinkins elevenses WR
foss waterfall
fost first
fo'tnit fortnight
fo'ty forty
fotch to fetch
fother to feed (stock)
foul (see **fahl**)
fower four
fowk people WR
frame to get organised; to show promise
frame thissen! get a move on! etc. (see p 40)
fratch to argue, disagree, quarrel etc.
fresh new; slightly drunk
frume(n)ty Christmas dish (see p 77)
fruzzins bits of thread or hair
fullock rush; blow
fun found
fust first
fuzzock donkey

gab mouth (of animal)
gadge man, fellow
gaffer boss; foreman
gallock-'anded left-handed
gallocker left-handed person
gallowa small horse, pony
gallusses braces for trousers
gammy lame, injured (leg etc)
gang to go NER
ganzey jersey, pullover
gat got
gate way
gaum heed; common sense
gaumless stupid
gawby a fool
gawk fool (see **gowk**)
gawp to gape, stare
gawp-'eead stupid person
gee back! right! (to horse)
gee up! faster! (to horse)
gerr away! I don't believe you etc
getten got
gey very NER
gi'en given
gill half a pint   ¼ pint = 5 oz.
gilt young sow
gimmer young female sheep
ginnel narrow passage between buildings
gip to feel to want to vomit
gip to gut fish
gird attack of pain or dizziness
girn to grin, pull a face
gitten (see **getten**)
gizzened choked (with emotion)
glass-alleys marbles made of glass
glazzoner sharp blow
gob mouth
gob-smacked speechless
goit channel of water
gollop to swallow greedily
gommeril fool

gooise goose WR
gooise-gobs (gogs) gooseberries
gowk cuckoo
goz, gozzle to spit
graave to dig
gripe fork
grovven dug
grundid buried
gumption common sense
gurt big
guytresh evil spirit (see p 77)

hahsummivver however WR
hallack to idle, dawdle
hame horse-collar frame
han'kercher handkerchief
happins bedding ER
harve! left! (to horse)
haver (pron **havver**) oats
haver-breead oatcake
hauf, hawf half
hawporth halfpence worth
heck! (see p 55)
heck rack; railings
heeam home NER
heft handle
hengments! (see p 55)
higg (see **'igg**)
hind farm worker; foreman
hippins baby's nappy
hoaf half NR
hoil hole WR
hollin holly
hooal hole NER
hooam home
hoss horse
hug, hugger to carry
huggin armful
huggins hips
hummer! (see p 55)

i' in
idle-back lazy person
'igg temper, huff; hurry

'igg, tak to take offence
ing meadow
intak(e) land enclosed from
  moors
'ippins (see hippins)
ivver ever

jannock fair, right
jart to hit
jerry (see **po**)
jibber horse refusing to move etc
jiggered exhausted, tired out
jinny-spinner daddy longlegs
jip severe pain
job often used in the sense of 'a
  bad job'
jock food (esp for a workman)

kak-'anded (see **cack-'anded**)
kali (pron kay-lie) sherbet
  powder
kall to gossip
kall-'oil place where people
  gather to gossip
kay-legged with crooked legs,
  knock-kneed
kelter(ment) litter, rubbish ER
ket rubbish, offal, carrion
kincough whooping cough
kist large box, chest (of drawers)
kittle to tickle; to have kittens
kittle tricky, tense, delicately
  balanced
kittlin kitten
knackers testicles
knap to snap; knock
knorp to knobble
knur hard knot of wood or ball
  used in game
kye cattle NER

laat to seek, search
lahle little
laik to play; to be unemployed

laikins toys
lair (see **laithe**)
lait (see **laat**)
laithe barn
lam to strike hard
land to give (a blow) (see p 64)
　arrive
lang long
lap to wrap (up)
larn to learn; teach
lat late; lath
lay to wager
lead to convey something (in a
　cart)
leeath barn NER
leet light
leet-gi'en simple-minded;
　fickle
leet on to meet by chance
lennick supple, limp, not stiff (of
　dead body) WR
let off (see **trump**)
let on to tell, reveal
lewk to look
ley scythe
leyke ti likely to NER
lief willingly (see p 64)
lig to lie, lay
ligger-aht woman employed to
　lay out bodies
liggin-in lying in (esp for
　childbirth)
likelins probably NR
likeness portrait, photograph
ling heather
lingy (see **lish**)
lip impudence, answering back
lish agile, lively, springy NER
lithin thickening
loin lane WR
lollicker tongue
look (see **lowk**)
lop flea
lose (see **lowse**)

loss to lose
lowance (see p 53)
lowk to weed
lowp to leap, jump
lowse to finish, close (school,
　mill etc)
lug ear; to drag, carry
luggy tangled (of hair)
luke (see **lowk**)
lye (see **ley**)

maddle to confuse, fluster
mafted stifled, flushed
mair more NER
maister master, boss;
　schoolmaster
mannishment manure NER
mardy spoilt (child); easily upset
marrer mate, friend; (see p 71)
mash to make, brew (tea)
maunce muddle, fuss
mawgrams, mak to pull a face
mawk maggot; surly, unfriendly
　person
mawngy surly, uncooperative
　etc
meeastlins mostly NER
mell to meddle; harvest supper
mend to get better (in health)
mengle mangle
mense decency, common sense
mense to tidy up
menseful decent, neat, thrifty
menseless senseless
mention a small amount
mester (see **maister**)
meyas mouse (part of WR)
meyt meat
mich much
mickle much, greater NER
middin dung-heap, dust-bin
middlin' moderate, average
　(esp of health)

mig muck, manure
mill-band (see p 77)
mistal cow-shed
mither muddle
moak donkey
moggie cat; **parkin** (qv)
moither to fluster, overwhelm etc
mooast almost
mother dee cow parsley
mowdiwarp mole
muck dirt, manure
muckment rubbish
muck-'oil dirty, squalid room or house
muck-rawk line of dirt (on neck etc)
mud might
muff the slightest sound
mullock mess
mun must

natter to irritate, annoy
nawpin free hand-out WR
nawther neither WR
neb nose, beak, front of cap
neean none NER
neeave fist
neet-rake one who stays up or out late
neet-soil soil used in privy
ner, nor than
nesh feeling cold; delicate
nessy outside lavatory, esp earth-closet
nimm to skip lightly, briskly
nip-screew miser, mean person
nithered very cold (of person)
nobbut only
nont aunt WR
nooan not; none
nowt nothing
nuggit nougat
nut not

oard old ER
ochin (see **urchin**)
ocker to hesitate
'od to hold
'od on! wait!
off-comed-un person from elsewhere
'oil hole, place WR (see p 54)
ollin holly NER
ommost almost
onnly only
onnyrooad anyway, however
'ooal hole, place NER
ooined harassed, hurt, depressed
'oss (see **hoss**)
owd old
ower over; to finish
own to recognise
owt anything
oxter armpit NER

pace egg Easter egg (esp rolled)
parkin gingerbread made with oatmeal
parky chilly
parzel to saunter, go cautiously
patten clog with irons on sole
patty fish-cake
pawse to kick
pays (see **peys**)
peggy tub large, barrel-shaped wash-tub
peff to cough (usually slightly)
penk to peer closely
pent engaged to finish piece-work
petty (see **nessy**)
pew-spice (see p 76)
peys peas
piggin lading-can; milking pail
piggy game hitting stick pointed at each end
pike (see p 53)
pine to go hungry, crave for food

pissimer, pissmire ant NER
pizeball game like rounders
pleeaf plough NER
ploo plough NER
plot neet, Bonfire Night WR
pluf plough NER
po chamber pot, under a bed
pobbies, pobs soft food, bread
 and warm milk
poise (see **pawse**)
poit poker
polled cut (hair etc)
pooak bag
posnit saucepan (esp with feet);
 bowl
poss purse ER
posser implement used in
 wash-tub (see p 53)
posser-'eead copper head of a
 posser
possit warm drink; milk brought
 up by baby
privy outside lavatory, esp
 earth-closet
proggin (see p 76)

queer as Dick's 'at-band very
 strange etc (see p 72)

rammle to wander, stroll; ram
rannle-bauk (see p 54)
ratch to stretch, exaggerate
ratten rat
rawk mist, drizzle
real splendid, wonderful etc
recklin weakest of litter
reckon to pretend; think; rod
 over fire for pans
reeasty rancid
reek (see **rick**)
reet, reight very
renny fox
reyk to reach
rheeubub rhubarb

rick smoke
rig back; ridge
rig-welted (see p 52)
rive to tear
rizzom tiny scrap, particle
rooad way
rooar to weep loudly
rops belly, guts (animals only!)
rud-stake (see p 52)

sackless ineffectual, silly etc
sad heavy, not properly risen (of
 bread, etc)
saig to saw
saim dripping; lard
sam (up) to gather, pick up
sarra to feed swill
scahr to scour (eg doorstep)
scale to rake, spread
scallions spring onions
scoddy meagre, poor (esp food)
scopperil spinning-top; lively
 child
scrat to scratch
seck sack
seea so NER
seeaminla apparently
seear sure NER
seeat seat WR; soot NER
seeaves rushes NER
seet sight; a great deal
seg small metal stud hammered
 into shoes; gelded animal
seggie second (children's games)
set-pot large copper for boiling
 washing (see p 53)
settle couch, sofa, seat
sewer, sewerly sure, surely
shackle wrist
shakked i' bits falling apart,
 mad, crazy
sharp quick
shepster starling
shibbands shoe-laces

shippon cow-shed
shiver very thin slice
sho'el shovel
shoo she
shoon, shooin shoes
showther shoulder
shun to ignore, not speak to
shutter to fall heavily (rain etc)
sich, sick such
sickened upset
sickened off repelled, put off
side to clear (eg pots from table)
sike(n) such
sile (dahn) to pour down (of rain)
sin since
sind to rinse
sipe to ooze, drain slowly
sitha! look (here)!
skeg glance
skelbeease (see p 52)
skelp to beat, thrash
skep basket; coal-bucket
skew-whiff cock-eyed
skrike to shriek
slaap slippery
slack with little work or business
slack coal dust and very small bits of coal
slack-jack lazy person
slack-set-up ineffectual, careless, etc (see p 53)
slack-wun'-up (see above)
slape (see **slaap**)
slart to splash
sluffened (see **'eart-sluffened**)
smit to mark sheep
smittle to infect (with a cold etc)
snap packed lunch (see p 53)
sneck latch
snicket passage-way, esp short cut
snig to drag out timber

snitch nose
snob cobbler
snod smooth
snook up to sniff up
sodger soldier
soft weak, cowardly WR; foolish NER
soss to drink
spanish liquorice
spawer visitor, tourist
spell splinter; rail
spice sweets
spice cake fruit cake, Christmas cake etc
spornin spurring
sprog to spit
spuggy sparrow
spurrins banns
staggarth stack-yard
stagnated taken aback ER
stalled fed up (with) tired of (something)
stang pole, shaft
starnel starling
starved very cold (of a person)
starved 'un one who easily feels cold
stattis hiring fair for farmhands, servants
stee ladder, stile
steeanchecker stone-breaker
steeane stone NER
steg gander
stell-hole gutter
stepmother-blessing sore skin near fingernail
stevvan to shout lustily
stirk bullock or heifer
stithy anvil
stoggy wood pigeon
stowp post NER
strickle to sharpen, hone
stot bullock; man in bright costume

strang strong NER
streea straw NER
sud should
suited pleased
summat something
sup to drink
swaal to throw (away)
swad pod
sweeal to melt ER; (see **swaal**)
sweet-cake plain (sweet) cake
swiddens patches of burnt
   heather

tack food
tally (see p 64)
taws marbles
teea toe NER
tee to tie
teem to pour, unload
tell-tale-tit tale-bearer
teng to sting
ter-morn tomorrow
tew to toil, struggle
tewit pewit, lapwing
thack to thatch
theeak to thatch
thible stick for stirring
thimmle thimble
think on to remember
thoil to be willing to give;
   to endure, tolerate etc
thrang (see **throng**)
threeap to argue; grumble,
   contradict
threng (see **throng**)
throit throat WR
throng busy
thropple throat
thruff through NER
thunner thunder
ti, tiv to NER
tide fair (see p 76)
tighten! get a move on! clear off!
   (see p 53)

tipple to topple
tipple dahn to pour down
tipple-tails somersault
ti(v) to NER
toathri several
tolther to hobble
tommy-roondhead huge stone
tommy-spinner (see
   jinny-spinner)
tonned turned NER
top coit overcoat WR
traipse to walk slowly,
   resentfully
traycle treacle
trig to fill
trollop slovenly woman
trump to break wind WR
tu'thri several
tul to
tumril wooden trough
tup male sheep
twilt to beat, thrash
twind to wind, turn, twist
twister textile term (see p 53)
twitchbell earwig
tyke dog, cur; Yorkshireman

'ug, 'ugger to carry
'uggins (see **huggins**)
ullot owl NER
'ummer! (see **hummer!**)
umpteen a lot
und (see **backside**)
urchin hedgehog
us our

varmint vermin
vast o' a lot of NER
varra, varry very
voider wicker clothes basket

waak weak
waffly shaky, dizzy
wahr worse

wahr war
wame (see **weeam**)
wang to throw
wankle weak, unsteady NER
wark work
wark ache
watter water
wed married
weeam stomach
weeant won't
wekken to wake
welt to hit
wemmle to overbalance
wengby leather; hard cheese
wer our
wether (see p 52)
weyver weaver
while until
whinny gorse
white-ovver/ower with a
covering of snow
wick life NER
wick lively, alive; quick (base of
fingernail)
wick week
winder window; to winnow
wint'r-'edge clothes-horse
wishin cushion
wisht silent
wockery weak
wolt to overbalance WR
wom home
wots oats NER

wrang, wreng wrong (esp
NER)
wurrum worm
wuthering wild, blustery,
howling (of wind) (WR
adjective made famous by
Emily Brontë)

yacker acre NER
yackrons acorns NER
yah one NER
yak oak NER
yal ale NER
yam home NER
yammer to chatter
yan one NER
yance once NER
yar one NER
yark to pull, esp with a jerk
yat gate; hot NER
yat-steead space for gate
yat-stowp gate post
yed head; yard
yell (see **bawl**)
yest yeast
yesterneet last night
yoller yellow
yond that, those; that person
yonder over there
yonderly with a far-away
look
yoon oven NER
yowe ewe NER

Bibliography

The English Dialect Dictionary (6 vols) (1905) by Joseph Wright
Survey of English Dialects Vol 1 (1962) ed H Orton and W J Halliday
The White Rose Garland (1949), a comprehensive anthology, ed W J Halliday and A S Humpleby
Yorkshire Dialect (1970) by J Waddington-Feather
The Yorkshire Yammer (1973) by Peter Wright
Keeping Yorkshire Alive (1977) verse by Hilda Stone
Poems from the Yorkshire Dales (1979) by Gordon Jefferson
East Yorkshire Miscellany (1981) by Jack Danby
A Levelheaded Deealsbred Lass (1988) by Ruth Dent
Cum thi Ways In (1990) by Ruth Dent (cassette also available)
East Yorkshire Facts and Fables (1990) by N Stockton
T' Lord's Mi Shepperd (1991) ed T M Cluderay

Publications by the Yorkshire Dialect Society

Emily Brontë and the Haworth Dialect by K M Petyt
An East Yorkshire Anthology ed Bill Cowley
A Cleveland Anthology ed Bill Cowley
An Anthology of West Riding Verse ed Gwen Wade
Dialect Verse from the Ridings ed. Bill Cowley *et al*
Humour from the Ridings, including poems by Geoffrey Robinson
Yorkshire Pudding Olmenack ed Ben Dyson and Stanley Ellis
Words throo t' Shuttle Ee ed Gerald England
The Muse Went Weaving by Fred Brown
Yorkshire at Work ed Peter Anderson
Selections from 'Goodies' ed Jack Danby and Muriel Shackleton

In addition the YDS publishes *Transactions* (ed Arnold Kellett) and *The Summer Bulletin* (ed Muriel Shackleton) as well as the dialect recordings *First o' T' Sort*, by various speakers, and *West Riding Tales* told by Arthur Kinder of Honley.

All YDS titles are available from the Librarian, YDS, School of English, the University, Leeds LS2 9JT.

Comprehension Test

To find an estimate of your percentage in the understanding of Yorkshire dialect, give the standard English of the following. Do not look anything up – or peep at the answers! (Overleaf.)

(a) Verbs

1. laik 2. pawse 3. bray 4. addle 5. fettle 6. lap 7. gang 8. kall 9. sud 10. rooar. 11 teem. 12. flit 13. lait 14. fratch 15. ammot 16. lowp 17. fun 18. smittle 19. lig 20. sind

(b) Adjectives

1. starved 2. druffen 3. capped 4. dowly 5. wick 6. brant 7. moithered 8. stalled 9. ooined 10. stagnated

(c) The Body and Clothes

1. een 2. lug 3. shackles 4. neeave 5. teas 6. gansey 7. 'ippins 8. brat 9. gallusses 10. shibbands

(d) Food

1. haver-breead 2. spice 3. frumenty 4. collops 5. peys 6. wengby 7. pobs 8. blegs/bummels 9. sweet-cake 10 spice-cake

(e) Creatures

1. hogg 2. gimmer 3. moak 4. mawk 5. lop 6. arran 7. buzzard 8. spuggy 9. stoggy 10 ullot

(f) Articles

1. cratch 2. posser 3. piggin 4. sneck 5. thible 6. kist 7. yat 8. stee 9. pooak 10. scopperil

(g) Places

1. mistal 2. bobby-'oil 3. closit 4. laithe 5. cham(b)er 6. shippon 7. delf 8. skeeal 9. midden 10. staggarth

(h) Phrases

1. Frame thissen! 2. Sam it up! 3. Side it! 4. Tha's shakked i' bits 5. Umpteen on 'em 6. Ah dursn't eyt it 7. Nobbut fower apiece 8. 'E's 'appen deeaf 9. A vast o' coos 10 Wi s'll wait while t' back-end 11. Ah'm nooan bahn yonder 12 T' chapils lowsin' 13 By gow! Tha'll cop it! 14. Ah'd as lief sup watter 15. Sitha! It's rikkin'! 16 Sh' wor fair 'eart-sluffened 17. Ah's bun yam 18. Onnyrooad, it's i' yon skep 19. Ah can't thoil it 20. It mud 'a' been wahr.

Answers to Comprehension Test

(a)

1. play 2. kick 3. hit 4. earn 5. fix, clean 6. wrap 7. go 8. gossip 9. should 10. weep 11. pour 12. move house 13. seek 14. quarrel 15. am not 16. leap 17. found 18. infect 19. lie 20. rinse

(b)

1. **cold** 2. drunk 3. surprised 4. miserable, poorly 5. alive, lively 6. steep 7. flustered 8. fed up 9. harrassed 10. taken aback

(c)

1. eyes 2. ear 3. wrists 4. fist 5. toes 6. jersey 9. nappies 8. apron 9. braces 10 shoelaces

(d)

1. oat-cake 2. sweets 3. Christmas dish 4. thick slices 5. peas 6. old cheese 7. bread and milk 8. blackberries 9. plain cake 10. Christmas cake

(e)

1. year old lamb 2. young female sheep 3. donkey 4. maggot 5. flea 6. spider 7. moth 8. sparrow 9. woodpigeon 10. owl

(f)

1. fireside chair 2. stick for wash-tub 3. small can or bucket 4. door latch 5. stirring stick 6. chest 7. gate 8. ladder 9. bag 10. spinning top

(g)

1. cowshed 2. police station 3. cupboard; toilet 4. barn 5. bedroom 6. cowshed 7. quarry 8. school 9. dung-heap; dustbin 10 stackyard

(h)

1. Get organised! 2. Pick it up! 3. Clear it away! 4. You're crazy! 5. A lot of them 6. I daren't eat it 7. Only four each 8. Perhaps he's deaf 9. A lot of cows 10. We'll wait until the autumn 11. I'm not going there 12. They're coming out of chapel 13. My word! You'll catch it! 14. I'd as soon drink water 15. Look! It's smoking! 16. She was quite heart-broken 17. I'm going home 18. Anyway, it's in that basket 19. I don't think it's worth spending the money on it 20. It might have been worse.

100-85 champion; 85-70 good; 70-55 varra fair; 55-40 nobbut middlin; 40-35 just fair 35-15 a bit of a job 15-0 a reight poor do!

Cranb